*Once an Adult,
Twice a Child*

Once an Adult, Twice a Child

❖

Alzheimer's Through a Caregiver's Eyes

Brenda Johnson

Copyright © 2014 by Brenda Johnson.

Library of Congress Control Number: 2014907815
ISBN: Hardcover   978-1-4990-0851-7
           Softcover   978-1-4990-0853-1
           eBook   978-1-4990-0850-0

All rights reserved. No part of this book may be reproduced or transmitted in any form or by any means, electronic or mechanical, including photocopying, recording, or by any information storage and retrieval system, without permission in writing from the copyright owner.

Any people depicted in stock imagery provided by Thinkstock are models, and such images are being used for illustrative purposes only. Certain stock imagery © Thinkstock.

Print information available on the last page.

Rev. date: 12/30/2014

To order additional copies of this book, contact:
Xlibris
1-888-795-4274
www.Xlibris.com
Orders@Xlibris.com
616585

Contents

Introduction 7

1. The Journey Begins 9
2. Challenges of All Sorts 28
3. A Place Called Home: Deciding to Close 51
4. Stories of Past Clients 75
5. Once an Adult, Twice a Child 96
6. Through the Caregiver's Eyes 125
7. Questions 151
8. Residence Inside of Me 171
9. Stuck in a Dream 191
10. Don't Be Alone 207
11. One Last Chance 224
12. How Did I Get Here? 242
13. A Little about Dementia 259

INTRODUCTION

This book is dedicated to all the families who have lost a loved one to Alzheimer's and dementia. I have spent over twenty-five years giving care to these moms and dads who have acquired this horrible disease. I'd like to take you on my journey and tell you about some of the experiences I've dealt with and some of the care I've done. Although some of these days and nights were hard, and sometimes I felt like running, never returning, I hung in there because I truly felt that this is my calling in life. There were a lot of tears, fears, smiles, and laughter; and no matter how sad or how hard times got, we could always find a moment for love. I hope that you will embrace my story and find some comfort as you read about all the challenges I encountered while giving care to those who could not care for themselves. May you find a little laughter as I take you through what some of you may view as impossible to go through. But unless you truly have a heart to give this type of care, it could never be for you; it can be greatly overwhelming. But for me, it is therapy—truly therapy. And this is why there are folks like me. It is my passion; I love to care for others. I hope you enjoy and find some comfort, smiles, and a little laughter as you go through this journey with me. I do not wish to be disrespectful or offend anyone by writing these short stories of actual accounts of some of the people I cared for. I'm writing in hopes you receive some insight on what it takes to be a great caregiver or how to find one. God bless.

Chapter 1

The Journey Begins

Around 1980, I was about eighteen years old when I went to New York City, leaving my three-year-old child behind. I had hopes of becoming a big star or a top fashion model and making a better life for the two of us. Well, I thought I had the looks and style to become either. But I kept running into takers who were scouting for young pretty girls like me who didn't have a clue, so I ended up working for agencies that gave me work, but I never saw a check. When I did, it was very small. I'm pretty sure they're raking in thousands for themselves. With low self-esteem, I just let go and walked away brokenhearted. One day, a friend who was caring for a bedridden elderly lady asked me if I would sit with this lady while she went to the market. I said sure. As I sat there talking to this poor soul who totally was dependent on someone to care for her, feed her, clean her—everything—I grew very sad. My heart so wanted to give to her I almost wished that somehow I could cure her, but I knew that this was impossible. So for the time that I was there, I catered to this lady as if she were my own mother or relative. She had my heart. I then knew that this was something that I wanted to do. I always had been a freehanded person who would literally give the shoes off my feet to save another's. It gave me so much joy and pleasure to help someone who couldn't help themselves. And the payback for me would be the smile on their faces, knowing that I was responsible for it. Oh, it's indescribable. I knew then that this was the job for me. This was something I wanted to do with my life, but I never took the time to become a nurse or even doctor. I guess back then I was confused and young. I also had a passion to serve the dead—yes, a mortician. Now don't run away or stop reading my book. It was just another interest of mine that I attempted to pursue. But when class time came, I didn't show up. I really believed that caregiving was my calling. Soon my friend got me hooked up with a care agency, and I got my first client to work with. I can't remember who she was since this was over twenty-five years ago. But I'm sure it was a joy. After working several jobs in New York and watching my clients pass away, I decided it was time to return home to Washington State where I continued as a caregiver.

Agencies

I started working for several agencies, mostly ones where I had to have three different clients in one day, spending about three hours at each home. I didn't really like that, but it was okay. I got to meet different people on a daily basis, only they all had different personalities, and they were just normal folks that needed housekeeping and errands mostly. It was fun talking to them, hearing stories of yesteryears and the life they lived long ago. I enjoyed getting the wisdom from them. Some could get very attached and would ask me to do things that were against agency policy, like spending the night. I had one guy try to get me to take him to the liquor store each time I showed up. Now that was a big, big no-no. I remember coming in one morning; he had already had a few for breakfast—drinks, that is. Well, these types of incidents must be reported, and the client would be notified to stop. If not, the caregiver could request to be removed. In that situation, if I did leave, it would have only gotten worse. You even had some agencies that really overlooked some regulations simply because they didn't want to lose the fee that that client was paying, and if they were private, it probably was a good amount of cash. Well, I moved on from him to another male client who was a hoarder, and I went right back to the agency to report this and to let them know that there was no way I was going to work in that mess. Well, he was called and told he had to clean it up before they would send me back there. After a couple of weeks, I was sent back, and there weren't mountains of trash anymore, but it still was very messy. I started to notice that this guy too had a taste for beer, and this job was pretty much not going to last. I think I stayed there about two weeks before it too was over. He couldn't wait to ask me to go to the store and buy him beer. I think I went once or twice. The agency made him an exception only because he was in a wheelchair. The more I complained, the more they ignored me and told me there were no more clients at the moment. I had rent to pay, so I had to stay until I could get another client. So day in and day out, I had to put up with this so-called veteran who was drinking himself to death and his dog who was as big as a horse and was far too big to be living in that small one-bedroom apartment. Each morning as I came in, I was faced with a hung-over guy in a wheelchair, mountains of empty beer cans and trash, and a huge dog that had peed all over the kitchen floor. Guess who do you think had to clean it up? Wooh! Did I get sick of that? You know what, after a while, I started to feel like this was my home, and I was the wife doing all the cleaning I had to complete in two and one-half hours. Wow, I wanted to just run. If that wasn't the tip of the iceberg, there was so much more than I could ever believe to come. I noticed that I was really starting to itch each and every time I got inside his home. As I confronted him about this, asking nicely if he could have fleas—and believe me I had never seen a flea in my life yet—he just looked at me for five seconds and then said, "Oh no, not that I know of." I informed him that I was really itching around my ankle areas. He insulted me by saying, "Gosh, I hope you didn't bring anything in here." Wooh! Again, ya'll know what I wanted to say, don't ya? But I had to maintain my composure, be professional, and let it go. I called the agency and told them, "Look, I've gotta get out of here. Something is eating at my ankles." They responded, "Did you ask him if he had fleas?" I responded back, "Yes, but what do they look like?" They described them so I could look out for them. I also told them another client or not, I would be leaving after I finished doing his dishes. As I continued my work, the dog came running in. I never pretty much gave the dog any attention; he kept him in the room with him. I decided to try to see if the dog had fleas on him, but how do you see fleas on a black dog? As I tried to look at the dog, I noticed his whole other side was eaten off and raw; this dog had fleas so badly you could nearly see his bones, and he was digging and scratching. Wow, that was it. I was out the door. I called the agency and explained to Bob why I was leaving and that I would be notifying the ASPCA. I couldn't believe the suffering that poor dog endured and what I could have as well. I believe I was put there to truly rescue this dog. God works in mysterious ways.

Tired of the Agencies

After working for many, many different agencies, I grew tired of all the driving from one person to another, so I sought out to find a private place to work where I could work with just one person each day. It was more of a bonding thing for me and definitely saved on gas and wear and tear of my automobile. So around 1994, I found a place that was an adult family home. This was really the first time I had heard of these private houses that people turned into somewhat private nursing homes for no more than six people per house, but it still wasn't what I was really looking for. So I met the owner of this home—Peggy, I'll call her. She was a nice lady. She took me and several other caregivers under her wing and pretty much showed us the ropes of the business. She paid for training in care classes; she really catered to us when it came to this business. At least that's how I felt about her. I took all that grooming in because I knew it would pay off for me one day because I loved this type of work, and I collected credentials through her that could open doors for me. That was as far as I could see right then. Peggy had opened several homes, and each of us worked in one, switching homes on some days. Although sometimes I got stuck caring for six people all alone when someone didn't come in to work, I still loved it. Pleasing these people and seeing their smiling faces after I cooked and cleaned them, conversed, laughed, and put them to bed—that said it all for me. It was hard-sweating work most times, but I still loved it. I was the type that loved to work out at the gym, so I basically looked at it as that. This type of work surely isn't for anyone. You've gotta have a passion for it, and I say passion because we're dealing with human beings, and you've absolutely gotta have respect for them and their bodies. After all, this is what you're going to be caring for. I've seen caregivers come and go because of burnout, especially when there's not enough help around. But for me, even though the adult family homes have six residents to each one, it did turn out to be a lot more fun for me. It wasn't the one-client setup that I wanted, but I was being settled in one place instead of driving all over town all day.

Peggy's Place

At Peggy's place, the residents got three meals and two snacks per day. The residents were pretty happy at that place or the home I worked in. I stayed in the same home instead of moving around like most other caregivers did, and finally I was made resident manager and lived on the premises with the residents. This meant getting up between 5:00 a.m. and 6:00 a.m. each day and getting the residents up to take baths, take medications, and eat breakfast. Usually a second caregiver would come in at or around 7:00 a.m. But since I was the resident manager, I was on duty twenty-four hours per day, even on my days off if someone didn't show (and believe me that happened quite a few times each week). That was because the home I worked in was a very heavy Alzheimer's care. Caregivers got burned out easily, and some just were there until an easier job somewhere else came along. So a lot of the time I had to give six baths, cook for six, give all six their meds, entertain six, chase after six, and do laundry and housekeeping for six. On most nights, I got to bed at midnight and be back up at 2:00 a.m., trying to get someone back into bed. By the time I got one back to bed, two more were getting up. Some were going back to the old place they called home, and others were simply confused and talking about yesteryears. They were little boys and girls in their minds and were up looking for their mommy or daddy. Some nights I'd sit and talk with whoever happened to be awake. We'd talk, and I'd help take them back to as much of their old lives as I possibly could, most of the time with tears welling up in my eyes. I wondered just how scary this must be for them and thought, *What are they really thinking about each day? Do they wake up frightened?* I can already see they are confused. I'll call her Anna. She was like clockwork. When I was up at approximately 3:00 a.m. each day, I could expect her for tea. She'd come in each morning crying, telling me about her mother who had just died. Mind you, Anna was ninety-two years old. I had just put someone back to bed and was quite tired, but I knew that to her this really had happened, and I had to console her. As we drank our tea, she'd tell me of how her mother died on that day, and she could not find her boyfriend and that she's gonna get rid of him because all he ever thought of was his penis. The laughter inside my head was overwhelming, but I had to maintain seriousness with her; as I said, this was actually real to her. As sad as it was, I wanted to be there for her as she grieved for her newly deceased mother.

Peggy's Place

Morning would come, and it was time to get busy once again. Each day was eventful. I can always expect an unexpected laugh or tear. But you keep going, recreating life for these poor souls who were searching to find their way basically in a land that is new to them. They were trying to get to the truth about what's really going on with them while running to a strange face that they thought was familiar to them and running away from one that should be. The loss of memory is a daily challenge to try to retrieve. They struggle to obtain old memories that used to be obtainable but were now long gone. It's just another day but with the same duties for me. Some will have visitors, and some won't have any and never do. That always broke my heart, especially around Christmastime. There would always be one or two left behind. No family would take them out for the day. On this day, I would always have some sort of Christmas dinner for whoever was left behind. I can remember two ladies that seemed to always have a tussle at dinnertime, taking each other's food. These two ladies had major Alzheimer's and required very heavy care. I will call them Martha and June. At dinnertime, I decided to sit in between these two ladies to try to stop them from taking each other's food. What did we have? Spaghetti. Usually the spaghetti was broken up into small pieces because for some residents, it was a struggle to eat. These two ladies also needed help with feeding, so as I turned to feed one, the other thought she would take this time to pour her plate over the top of my head. What could I do but laugh? But what was even funnier was the fact that as I looked up, everyone thought it was funny and was laughing. It was so amazing to me that these people couldn't feed themselves or put their clothing on properly or remember a face, but they somehow could see that the spaghetti on top of my head was funny. So we all continued to laugh about it, and till this day, I am still wondering, *Was that just some kind of short-term-memory thing?* Simply amazing. Some of the ladies seemed to like to and could remember setting the table. So I would involve as many as I could around dinnertime to help put out the plates and napkins, and most times they did a great job.

Peggy's Place

So my job as a caregiver at Peggy's place went on for about two years or so. I watched caregivers come and go. No one could do it as great as I could. Since I was the resident manager, I was always very particular of how the residents were dressed, cleaned, etc. Some caregivers had to be continually reminded of how to give baths and medications. After a while, it got to be quite repetitious and old. Things just weren't being done quite right. I would usually come in and find the work that was supposed to be done when my shift started unfinished or undone, so I'd end up doing my work and everyone else's. So I decided then that I didn't want people there that weren't helping or doing the care for these folks. At that point, being a first-time negotiator, I was doing all the care. Since the owner had a few problems, I thought that this would be a great time to ask her to let me take over, especially since she had five other homes up and running. At first she told me I wasn't ready experience-wise. I had been there for two years, taking care and managing this place. Why couldn't I own and run it? I was more than experienced. I did all the paperwork, care, shopping, medication ordering, etc. I was more ready than she would have known. So I heard she offered another caregiver an opportunity to buy one of her homes, and someone put a good word in for me. It was a really good deal for me. I had a business already set up. Only I now had to get the license in my name. This took about thirty heart-pounding days, and finally, I got it. I had my own business and immediate income. I felt as if I hit the lottery. Wow, I'm a business owner. Things were going quite well. I treated everyone as if they were my own children, but burnout was not far behind, and I didn't just want anyone caring for my children. Although we know that they were far from being children, this was how I felt, and you could always count on them acting as children most times. I was so afraid of not finding someone to work and care for these folks, so I just did everything by myself for about one year. I eventually trusted my son and his girlfriend to help every now and then, but this was not their cup of tea, and one of their friends really didn't work out. But I knew my son wouldn't let me down for the short time that they did help. It seemed that every time I took a break, within the hour, I'd be right back. No one seemed to be able to care for these folks. They all claimed it was too much. They just weren't a caregiver at heart, and as I said, you've really gotta have this in your blood. It was my passion.

Brenda's Place: A Place Called Home

So a Place Called Home was born, and my journey of having my own care home was finally realized. I saw to it that these moms, dads, grandpas, grandmas, friends, aunts, and uncles had someone that would not only be there for them but would also be the voice that they could no longer be. I chose the name A Place Called Home because that is what I wanted to give to these folks: a place they could truly call home and not feel as though they were in an institution or a nursing home. This would truly be their home. I wanted to be one of the first to make a big difference in these folks' lives. So many of them had been abused and thrown around from place to place, trying to find the care they deserved; and when they did get to my place, they could truly feel they were at home and could expect to be there until the end of their lives. These folks don't really have too much to look forward to day in and day out, so I would create some sort of activity that they could take part in, but most times the attention span did not last. So I always made up for it by making dinners special. A few candles lit and classical music always seemed to catch their attention, and most times everyone was calm and quiet during mealtime. They seemed to really enjoy this. No one knew that there were to be no candles lit in the household, but as long as they didn't know, I was going to make dinnertime as special and as fun as I possibly could. There would always be someone trying to tell a story of yesteryear at dinnertime. I think the candles may have sparked a memory of long ago, perhaps a favorite restaurant, a birthday party, or a candlelit dinner at home with their loved one. I always wondered about that. I always loved to burn candles. Even one candle just seemed to bring some sort of instant peace through the house, especially on a cold night with a hot cup of tea. These folks loved to have hot chocolate before bed at night—well, most of them. We always had a snack before bedtime, but I could usually count on someone getting up two hours later.

Sundowners Nights

Sundowning is a disorder when people with Alzheimer's get their days and nights mixed up; therefore, they would pack away, hide, and go through all their things and, a lot of times, someone else's things through the night. There would be nights when someone would come out with three pairs of pants, two pairs of socks, and two blouses on. Most of the time, they had forgotten that they put a garment on already. When sundowners happen, you really need two or three caregivers on duty. You can look forward to being up most of the night. Then they want to sleep during the day. So you can imagine the exhaustion I felt a lot of mornings after being up all night, getting by on three hours of sleep and being the only caregiver on duty. People asked me how I did it. I would tell them, "I think I was having an out-of-body experience most times." I really don't know how I got through that. Don't really ever attempt to try to reason with a person who has advanced Alzheimer's about getting a layer or two of their clothing off. It will be a losing battle. You may even find yourself ducking. They sometimes may become very combative and are very protective of their things—clothing, hats, food, even their dentures or someone else's dentures. There was an incident. I will call her Janet. Janet's dentures went missing, and I couldn't find them anywhere. That's another trick: they could hide things, making them disappear into thin air. So I decided that the family should probably get her fitted for another upper plate. Poor Janet found it hard to believe at times to eat without both parts of her teeth. We had more than one person in the house that was possessive of their things, and I will call her Betty. These two ladies shared a room, so this is why this loss of dentures happened. One happy morning, while everyone sat eating their breakfast, I noticed that Betty's mouth looked just a little twisted and pushed forward. But that didn't stop her from eating. After all, eating was one of her hobbies. After dinner, I escorted her to the bathroom to clean her dentures with the intention of really trying to see if they were Janet's. She gave me a short fight to get them, but when I did, I clearly could see that they were Janet's teeth and her name was engraved on the inner side. It was very funny, but Janet finally got her teeth back. Even the caregiver should hide their things. When a person has Alzheimer's in the middle to late stages, they really are like three-year-olds. They are busy, busy, busy; and you will be constantly on your feet serving them.

The Late-night Chase

I took in a lady on a temporary basis; her daughter had an emergency and needed a place to drop her mother for two days. She seemed to be a quiet little lady, but upon her daughter leaving, she became very antsy and wondered when she would be picked up. I constantly told her that her daughter would be back for her very soon. She quieted down, and I thought that I would get her ready for bedtime. While unpacking her things, I thought that she was washing up in the bathroom. Well, she was still sitting in the living room. Finally, I got her to come to the bedroom and get undressed for bed, but she refused and said, "Oh no, my daughter will be back shortly. I'll just stay dressed." No matter what I said, she just refused to change into her PJs. So I decided I'd let her just stay in her clothing for that one night; maybe she needed to feel comfortable first. As she got into bed and I turned out the lights and said good night, I thought everything would be okay. About one hour later, I decided to go down and check on her, and just in time, I caught her opening up the window on her way out. Before I could get to her, she was out and jogging down the street. I couldn't believe my eyes. This eighty-five-year-old lady was actually jogging down the street at 11:00 p.m. I somewhat panicked on what to do, but I had to get her back inside of the home. I didn't think of calling 911 at that time. I was so consumed with just getting her back into the house. Everyone else was sleeping peacefully, so I decided that I would go after her. This little lady could go. When I caught up to her, I tried to get her into the car. She told me to go on back and that she was walking to her daughter's house up on Twelfth Avenue, which was nowhere in the area. Finally, I had to get out of the car to talk her into getting in. One hour later, she was inside, but I had to tell her that her daughter was waiting at the house, and we must hurry and return before she leaves. That was the ticket; she was ready to go. But now I was stuck with what to tell her once we got back and her daughter was not in sight. This was quite the cleverest little lady I had ever seen. So I had to call the house with another phone, pretending that her daughter was on the other line, and I told her that I must tell her daughter of her actions tonight. Oh, that did it. She pleaded with me not to tell her. I acted as if I were speaking to her daughter and told her I'm gonna try to see if I could get her back into bed and that I would call her if there were any other problems and that

I was sorry that she could not make it tonight. We would be looking forward to her return the next day. Finally, after all the sneaking and fake phone calls, I got her back into bed; and from midnight on, I was the late-night watch woman. I just wished I had made sure all windows were locked. This particular room needed that window lock repaired. I didn't think I'd get someone in there that soon. This little lady had Alzheimer's, but I also think she had some unmentioned mental issues. In this field of work, you're the doctor, mother, babysitter, and sometimes even a counselor. You never ever know what to expect. But as I look back at some of the incidents and tests, they still hold lots of laughter and happy thoughts in my mind with all my children.

The Caregiver in Training

Well, as I said before, I really didn't have too much help with the care of my folks, so I hired another caregiver who I thought would be just great. I would get her the training she needed as a live-in caregiver like how I started out. This caregiver was around the same age as I was, so I knew that we would work great together because we were two mature ladies, and we would respect these folks like they should be. So the first week went good, and the second, and the third was even better. At this point, after not really having a break since taking over this home, which was months, I thought that I could now probably take a break and get some rest, take a night off, go to a nice hotel, and just sleep, catch up on my rest. This is what I did. I made sure that this caregiver had everything in order. I handled some of the more important tasks before I left for my hotel. As you already know, I treated these folks as if they were my own children. So once I got settled at the hotel, I decided to call and check on everything. Everything was good. At this time, it was around 10:00 p.m., and everyone was fine, so I decided to order a late dinner for myself and go on to sleep. But for some reason, I only tossed and turned just the same way a mother would if she was worried about her newborn baby. Around midnight, my gut kept saying, "Get up and go check on your people." After paying $150 for a very nice room, I decided I'd rather be back at home with the residents to ensure all was fine. This was a pretty huge home with up-and-down stairs and chandelier-type lights hanging over the large deck off the living room. I wondered why they were on that time of night. I figured maybe the caregiver was afraid, being there basically alone. But as I drove down into the garage area, I noticed that the entire house was lit up. I thought, *What was she doing? Up watching movies? What was going on here?* So I rushed inside calling out to her and got no answer. I then got bubble guts. I knew she was not there; my instincts were right on, especially when I heard a resident yelling for help. She left, stealing about $1,700 in cash and some of my clothing, and one resident was on the floor with soiled undergarments on. Sick was not the feeling I felt. It was more like I'm going to faint. Oh god, she robbed me and left these people to fend for themselves. Thank god for a woman's intuition. Careful who you hire. Be as thorough as you can before you hire someone. Always check out the works even if you know them.

Chapter 2

Challenges of All Sorts

Sometimes our folks with Alzheimer's are moved into a different home. It usually takes a while for them to realize that they are going to have to remain in their new home, and most times after they've been there for a while and have settled in, they become possessive about sharing the home with others living there. Usually they begin to think that they are the sole owner of the home and end up trying to boss everyone else around, even the caregivers. This will lead me to tell you a story about a little lady whom I shall call Lea. On this wonderful evening, everyone had dinner outside on the deck. And the evening went just great! I got everyone to stay seated, and I really think that they enjoyed dining outdoors for a change. It was getting close to bedtime, so we had to wrap up dinner when everyone had finished. I got everything cleaned up and everyone off to bed. I was so grateful that this evening went off without one really bad challenge. Believe me, there is usually more than one daily. I thought I'd relax for one-half hour or so before doing my daily activity reports and go off to bed myself. As I relaxed outside, I noticed that it was starting to drizzle a little, and I had better get in before the big rain started. Wouldn't you know it that as I went to the door, it was locked. Oh my gosh, what am I gonna do? No one could hear me, and most of the bedrooms were down the hall off the living room. The people that slept upstairs really couldn't understand anyway—well, no one except Lea. The rain started to pour, and I was quickly getting soaked. The only thing I could attempt to do was climb over the railing. Mind you, I was up on second level, and the way this home was built, that was higher than average. So it was climb over and try to get Lea's attention or spend the night outside. So I started to climb over onto the ledge. Wow, was I scared, and it was slippery. I could see Lea lying in her bed sleeping, but I had to hurry and tap on her window before I fell. That would of at least cost me a broken leg or two. I finally got her attention, and she came over to the window. Was I happy. I said, "Lea, honey, it's me, Brenda. Please come to let me in. It's raining, and I'm stuck outside." She said, "Who? What do you want?" Once again, I said, "Lea, it's me, Brenda. Please come and unlock the door." She responded, "I'm not gonna do it! Who are you?" I knew right then that I may be spending the night out in the pouring rain. She didn't remember me that quickly. If I could only get her to open the curtain so she'd see my face, she may recognize that it was me. So I persuaded her to come over to the window, and once again, she asked, "Who are you?" At this point, I was really getting a little upset, and I was soaked and cold. Finally, she said, "Oh, you." And I watched her walk out of her bedroom. I prayed she was not going to the bathroom but coming to rescue me. There she was coming around the corner straight to the door and quickly unlocked it. It was so fascinating how for those few minutes she didn't recognize me. I then knew that her Alzheimer's was taking another turn. Surprises all the time. But I did get dry and to bed. This disease is very tricky at times. Lea did think this was her home. How could she let this stranger in her home? But lucky for me, her short-term memory kicked in.

Alzheimer's versus Mental Illness

Although some of these stories about my caregiving days, real experiences, and trials may seem a little too much to take—or maybe not—at any rate, I hope that you will see and try to understand that I am truly trying to bring this to you as live as I can in hopes that you will and can visualize what goes on in the days and nights of a caregiver for people with Alzheimer's, dementia, and sometimes mental illnesses. Let me tell you the story of Larry. Now most times if there is space available and you have the training, you may have multiple people in your home with different illnesses. Now before I took Larry into my home, I first thought I should meet with and talk to him to see exactly what his needs were, especially since he was a mental illness client and I was really used to Alzheimer's and dementia clients. Why did he want to come to my home? I went to the mental hospital to meet with Larry. Larry appeared to be a very nice man who had a stroke, so he wasn't very verbal. I sat and tried to talk with Larry and his counselor who informed me that Larry was better and was ready to be in an adult family home setting. I had no experience with a person like him, so I didn't know what to expect, but I was told that he was a good person that didn't want to be institutionalized any longer. My heart went out to Larry, and I could understand him not wanting to be there any longer. So I negotiated a plan that would allow Larry to be there in my home for a period of thirty days, and if I could not accommodate him at any time before the thirty days were finished, he would be sent back to the mental institution. So they agreed, and the next week, arrangements were made for him to come to my home. Larry was great for the first thirty days, and on day thirty-one, he decided that he would show me what mental illness really was and let the games begin. Larry was very demanding, something I wasn't told. Larry would throw violent tantrums if he didn't get his way or food that he was not allowed to eat since he was a diabetic. Larry was disruptive at the dinner table, frightening the other residents. Larry knew how to play the game well. It was past the thirty days, so I could no longer just take Larry back to the institution. I thought, *My god, what have I done?*

Alzheimer's versus Mental Illness

I called the institution, trying my hardest to bring Larry back, but the contract stated no. I told them how Larry was acting and that I could not handle him. He was really starting to be disruptive. Anyhow, I ended up having to find a place for him myself. I looked high and low, and no one would take Larry. I couldn't even find a place that kept people with mental illnesses. So I decided that I would just try to work with him. Wow, was this a trial. I did total care for Larry. This meant bath, shave, haircut, and nails. He could feed himself. He did receive the pampering from me. This was my way of establishing some sort of relationship with him in hopes of calming him down a bit when he wanted to throw his tantrums. The other residents didn't care for Larry too much. He really started to demand most of my time, and I had to try to get him to understand that he was not the only one in the home and that I was one person sharing my time with everyone there. He seemed to understand at that time. Well, it wasn't too long before he decided it was time to test me again. On this night, we were having baked pork chops for dinner, and Larry was not allowed to have any pork; but I made sure that his meat was just as delicious as everyone else's, which was beef tenderloin. But so what? Larry wanted and insisted on the pork. But I told him once again no, so he decided he would throw a tantrum and toss his entire plate across the room and beat his fist on the table. Well, I can tell you that I was taken aback. He started to yell and shake himself in his chair. All I can say is that Larry was rushed and whisked away from the table to his bedroom for the remainder of the evening. Oh yeah, he yelled for about one hour until he realized no one would give in to his fits. I was told that this man could not walk, and by bathing him, I saw that all he could do was help transfer a little by just standing but no walking. I guess he planned to show me that he could walk, around 2:00 a.m. It's funny now. In hindsight, as I turned over in my bed early that morning, I could see someone standing over me. My first thought was someone had broken in, and they were breathing very hard. Was I scared? I just decided I'd go and turn on the lamp, and guess who? It was Larry standing over me, breathing very rapidly, with red marks all over his face. I said, "What are you doing in here, Larry? How did you get in here?" They told me he could not walk at all. But this man got out of his chair and walked over to my bedroom. This was really shocking and scary for me. I didn't know what to think or what he was thinking either. Were the red spots a reaction to something? 911 was called. They kept him overnight, and at 3:00 a.m., I was immediately up and waking people up, trying to place Larry. I was so afraid at this point. He just had to go. He had no family, but he did have a friend who somewhat cared for him. I told her what happened and that I didn't feel safe with him in the home anymore and that he had to leave ASAP! She came the next day to help. To make the long story short, two months later, Larry was placed in a group home; and as for myself, I could finally go to sleep at night and finally shut the other eye when I was going to sleep. You gotta be more careful. They don't always give you the full story.

The Passing of Jim

A good friend of mine asked me if I would take her ex-husband in if I had an extra room. I said sure, after placing Larry elsewhere. I will call him Jim. Jim was a very tall handsome man. But he didn't have Alzheimer's; he was just sick with a rare type of brain cancer and didn't have very long to live. I didn't really get all the facts on the type of cancer exactly, but I was told it was rare. If you could look at the top left of his head, you could see that Jim had a lump in the shape of an egg just sitting there on his head. Oh, my heart went out to him so very much. After all, he was about the sweetest man you could ever meet. Jim would sit in the La-Z-Boy and wink at me all day as I went along doing my chores. I thought it was very cute of him. And the sympathy I had for this family was as if they were my own family. His youngest son would come over nearly every night to see his dad. Poor fellow, I felt so sorry for him; he was very nice. But after each visit, he'd come out of the bedroom sobbing like a two-year-old. Oh, it was so hard for me to see this grown man cry. He'd always make me cry, and I'd comfort him by hugging him and telling him that his dad would be okay and that God has him in his hands. That seemed to always make him feel better. Each day Jim got worse and was in severe pain. But he had a doctor's order for morphine to keep him comfortable. The place he had come from didn't really take care of him at all. Jim was going down very rapidly and was very thin. I did my very best to give him the best care I could. Soon Jim was confined to his bed; and I'd bring his meal in, feed him, and do all personal hygiene for him from his bed. I could see that Jim was very sad. So I decided that reading a good book to him daily would help to make this journey a little easier. Each day a different book, each day a brighter smile he'd give me. I got comfort from this man, and I was pleased that he cared enough to get to know me. Even though I was there to care for him, I learned a lot from this dying man. And I hope that he learned a little from me too. On a Monday morning after getting the other residents fed, washed up, and comfortable, it was time to attend to Jim. I did really look forward to caring for him. After cleaning him up and feeding him, I picked another spiritual book to read to him. On this day, Jim was in a lot of pain and not smiling too much. I could see that his time would come soon. So I held his hand and tried to read to him without him noticing me crying. As I read on, Jim always had his eyes closed. It was getting close to lunchtime, and I needed to hurry to get lunch ready for everyone. As I continued to read the story, I realized that Jim was no longer there and probably had passed on for the last five minutes or so. As I checked his breathing, I confirmed that he had gone. It was such a sad time for me as I let go of his hand and said good-bye. I now had to find the strength to call his family and let them know of his passing. It was especially hard because I had to see his youngest, who was very close to his dad. As I got lunch for the others and waited for the family to arrive, I struggled not to alarm the other residents. But it wasn't long before the youngest came running through the door with his face soaked and wet. The residents then knew something was wrong. I comforted the family best I could and went through the remainder of the day not with sadness on my face but with a smile every time I looked at the chair Jim used to sit in. I remembered the winks he'd give me and that beautiful smile and said to myself, "There will be someone just as beautiful as him, waiting in heaven to brighten each day. Good-bye, Jim. You were a great man. You will be missed. Your friend, Brenda."

Another Death, Another Sad Day

When Maggie came to my home, she was walking but had been affected by a stroke that prevented her from speaking properly, and she also had Alzheimer's. Maggie was, I have to say, a very mean lady; and it showed all over her face. She didn't really get involved with anyone; she really didn't even want to be involved with me, but she knew that I was the one who had to care for her, so she did open up to me. She would try to speak, but it was mostly loud mumbling. Maggie loved to eat, but her meals had to be pureed (put through the blender). She could no longer chew foods, and she was on a thickener to allow her to swallow easier. Maggie liked to walk around and I'd say to pick on the other residents. She'd pull their hair. If they had food, she'd grab it. She can be compared to a very hyper four-year-old, I'd say. If she didn't get what she wanted, you could be sure she'd let out a loud mumble to let you know she wanted something. After having Maggie for about six months, her health went down very quickly, and she could no longer walk and had to be in a wheelchair. But this did not stop her from going after the other residents. She still would roll over to someone and try to bite them with her gums or take their things. At times, she was very funny. There was a time when we were all just sitting around watching the television, and Maggie was always sitting next to me to protect the other residents. All of a sudden, Maggie reached over and grabbed my arm. I think she thought that she was actually putting her teeth into my skin in her mind, but what she was actually doing was gumming my arm. This lady, at about eighty-nine years old, was so strong. She had a grip on my arm, and it took some time to get free from that grip. I always wondered what was going through her head. Did she think my arm was food, or was she just mean and wanted to bite me? Over a few more months, Maggie's health went down even more until she was confined to her bed, and she became total care. Each morning, I would get Maggie up and put her in her chair for breakfast.

Because of her swallowing problem, it was better to have her sitting up. The other residents seemed to always just stare at Maggie. I think the two in the house who could still communicate a little wondered what was going on with her. Sometimes Maggie would look over at them and stick her neck out and yell at them but in a mumbling fashion. This fascinated me because I knew that whatever it was she was saying to them, it wasn't very nice. I would sit next to Maggie at quiet time; and she would look me in the face and mumble, mumble, mumble. I always knew that she was having a conversation with me, but I have no idea what she was saying. So I'd just shake my head and say oh yeah. At least this made her feel that I was listening to her. As I went to prepare Maggie's breakfast one bright and sunny morning, I told her I'd be right back and to hold on. When I returned, just like that, that quick, Maggie had passed on. She was right there in her chair, gone. Although death never bothers me, it never ceases to amaze me. One minute here and gone the next, in the blink of an eye, and you know what? You don't have to have Alzheimer's for it to happen. Have you ever heard someone say, "I just saw her yesterday"? That's what I was saying. My gosh, she was just here, and now she's gone just that fast. I guess we've all got that final date with death. So please take care of where your soul ends up.

Jealousy Issues

Well, as you know, most people with Alzheimer's act like children most of the time. They fight over things, like clothing, food—anything they may think was theirs—while they were in their own home. I've even found out that they would fight for the attention of a person, and that person was me. I'll call this gentleman Paul. Paul was one of the first persons that was at my home. As a matter of fact, he came with the home. He was there when I became owner of the place. Paul was a veteran and loved to watch John Wayne movies, and his favorite meal was Subway sandwiches and chips. Paul also loved to smoke; he smoked so much that I had to soak his fingertips at the end of the day because they were stained with nicotine. He was what you would call a real chain-smoker: light one up and take that filter and light up another, back to back. Paul got a lot of my attention in the beginning, so I think that he somehow thought that he had all rights to me. After other residents came, I could no longer just focus on him alone, so I think he got pretty jealous over not getting my full attention anymore. There were times when I would leave, and he'd give the caregiver a very hard time. I could always come back and get the full report of him not cooperating—no eating, not anything. I was told that he would just sit there with his arms folded and angry at the world. But as soon as I returned, he was all smiles. There was a time when I had an evening meeting, and I had to wear a dress. As I told all the residents good night, Paul took it upon himself to ask where I was going, what time I would be back—oh, and here's the kicker. He told me to take off the dress and that I was not going out in a dress. At first I thought it was funny and cute. I thought he was he was just joking. But oh no, he quickly let me know that he was not joking and threw a very bad tantrum. I could not believe my eyes, especially that he was usually a quiet person. He was so upset that he slid himself out of the wheelchair onto the floor. This was his way of trying to get me to stay home. But I quickly let him know that this was not gonna work and that he should let us get him back into the chair and off to bed. After getting him settled down, I left him with the caregiver. I must have been gone for two to three hours. After 10:00 p.m., Mr. Paul was still sitting up with arms folded. He refused to go to bed and insisted on waiting for my return. After having a short conference with the caregiver, she told me about his night, and he was not very nice to her at all. So I told her she could go home and I would get Paul into bed. I felt like a child who had climbed out of her window to be with a boyfriend, and Dad was waiting up for me. I just went and told Mr. Paul it was bedtime, and we would discuss his behavior in the morning. His last words to me were next time he would make sure I didn't leave him with a caregiver. My response was firm. "Paul, you are not my husband or keeper. Now go to bed, and I don't want you to ever be disrespectful like that again." He refused to go to bed, and he meant it. So I informed his relatives about his behavior for that night and let them know that he spent the night sleeping in his wheelchair since he refused to be put to bed. I couldn't believe my eyes. Lesson learned. Sometimes it's not good to get so close to your residents. In Paul's case, his mind took him back in time, and he really believed I was his wife. You never know what will happen in this line of work, and work it truly was.

Wanting to Be Number One

Although I was new to this business, but not caregiving, I thoroughly enjoyed it. I'd say it was my calling. I ran a very strict and clean home. These residents were my children, and they were so special to me. Everyone that came to visit and even the inspector would comment on how beautiful and tidy my home was, and they couldn't figure how I could do it—care for everyone like cook, clean, give their medication, do the paperwork, wash their clothes, give them baths, and sometimes provide entertainment. As I always said, you've gotta love it, and it's certainly not for everyone. I even had a couple that was in love with the home so badly that they tried to talk me into selling. To be honest, they got me a little upset. They came there telling me one thing. But I quickly found out their intentions were to try to get my home. Wow, people always amaze me, and some of the things they'd come up with were just crazy. At one time, I had a waiting list, thanks to a social worker putting the word out on my home. It had always been my goal to try to have one of the best homes around, and I quickly did get that reputation. There were so many bad homes around; and some of the stories you'd hear simply were unbelievable but true, with people being abused, beaten, and disrespected. All this made me so sick inside. Didn't these folks know that they were gonna be old one day and that could possibly be them or even their mom, dad, or relative? My gosh! Some people just don't think. They think they will live forever and not ever grow old. It seemed that every time I got the chance to watch the news, there would always be a story about someone's mom or dad walking away from their care home and getting lost and authorities finding them days later cold and more confused. I used to always wonder what was on that caregiver's mind. Were they sleeping? Nine times out of ten, that was the case. A lot of caregivers are poorly screened and trained and hired out of desperation, usually causing some horrible accidents. And who takes the fall? The owner. You'd think they'd be more careful about the stability of their business. But I must be honest. As sad as it is, this business is supposed to be about caring for our elderly in their golden years. Forgive me. I must be so bold to say everyone wanted money and was just pimping the elderly. Ooh, that just got me so hot and angry. In the beginning, it was a nice business, and the few people in it were so happy to be serving our elderly. Somehow all the people who were greed stricken found out about it, and the licenses were getting handed out like candy. You had people from all walks of life opening up care homes, and what was so sad is they didn't have one clue about how to care for these folks in the place they chose to call home. There was no love, concern, care, or integrity about the place that their family selected for them. They too got fooled. I'm so glad that the state got hold of the regulations and made it a little hard to just come in and open one of these places. Some people couldn't even speak English. Till this day, I wonder just how they passed the test and got a license. United States of America, what are we doing? As I approach the elderly years in my life, I try to set aside my fears and pray that I won't need the services of a care or nursing home. And if so, please let it be one of integrity, with lots of respect, cleanliness, and awesome caregivers.

Alzheimer's in America

Next to cancer, Alzheimer's is one of the most feared diseases around. And I guess it probably is because with Alzheimer's, there's total brain failure. A person becomes unable to do the basic life skills right down to forgetting his or her loved one's name. Can you imagine waking up one day and not knowing who you are or how to put on your clothing, forgetting your name? Scary! I can't imagine it. Even though I've seen it day in and day out for years, it is still hard for me to imagine myself getting like that. It always happens to someone else, doesn't it? There are a couple of things that I can imagine, and that's how they may feel: the confusion, the sadness, and the feeling of being alone. It's as if you're all by yourself, even though your close family may be coming around. You're still lonely, mainly because you no longer know them. You want to talk to someone and ask what's really wrong with you, but you're too afraid to ask because everyone keeps telling you that you have this dreaded disease, and you really don't want to hear that because your mind tells you that they are only lying to you. More confusion and sadness set in because you wonder why they would want to tell you such a thing. And now you really look at them as an enemy, and I really feel that this is why a lot of people with Alzheimer's become violent and combative. There's a struggle going on within, and they are afraid to turn to anyone. Even their best friend is no longer recognized. In the next few years, if the government doesn't get a grip on finding a cure or better medications for this disease, most insurance companies will go bankrupt. Then we will have thousands walking around with no health care and nowhere to turn, just walking the streets unable to care for themselves. Now this will be a total disaster and really scary. Can you imagine thousands walking around not knowing where they're headed and unable to keep themselves clean? That is really something to think about and not just for your mom or dad or relative. I'm talking about the whole nation. The United States is not the only one facing this dilemma. Imagine this: You're caring for your mom, who you love dearly and would do anything for. One day she was just struck with Alzheimer's, and she had no health insurance, and you're working a nine-to-five schedule each day, barely making ends meet yourself. What would you do? Where would you go? Just take a moment and really think about that. How would you get her the care she needs? The average cost for a nursing home stay is approximately $10,000 per month, depending on the care level, and sometimes they don't even get proper care. Depending on the nursing home, most people don't even really care about this disease. Oh, they hear about it and are somewhat puzzled by what they've heard. But they really don't have all the facts on just what effects it has on a person. It would never be them anyway. I've even seen people sit and laugh about how someone they knew had Alzheimer's and that it was somehow God's way of getting back at that person. All I had to say quietly in my mind about them was be careful how you view and say what God has done to someone. Just be careful. Although I must say that people with Alzheimer's can do and say some very funny things, by no means at all would I say that the disease itself is funny and that God did that to a person. It's such a sad and lonely thing inside the mind of someone with this disease. Being around these folks has taught me so very much to care for them day in and day out. One of the most important is to enjoy your health. If you are blessed enough to have great health at this time, be so thankful. It could turn in a blink of an eye. Today is a gift. Unwrap it slowly and enjoy!

Why I Tell

I tell you stories about some of the folks that I've cared for over the years because I not only took care of these folks but I also had my own family members who were stricken with this disease. I can remember telling people how diabetes is really getting around quickly, and it still is. But I'm hearing so much about Alzheimer's more than ever before, especially in people I never thought would ever get something like that. But life is funny like that—and special. You never know what's just around the corner. The mind is really a terrible thing to waste. That's why we must eat right with lots of fruits and vegetables, not so much red meat. Please leave out the preservatives, sweets, and things like that. But you know, I've seen people live a reckless and careless life and outlive us all (go figure). I never could understand how or why those things happen. Some people just abuse their poor bodies till hell freezes over and they are still around. When the jogger, and biker, that rode his bike thirty miles a day, the swimmer, the runner, all these health fanatics, doing everything right. And the next thing you hear is they have the worst disease out there. They're dead and gone; but that smoker, drug addict, crack smoker, and IV drug user for twenty-five years or more are still around, enjoying doing more drugs, cigarettes, and alcohol. I've always had this question for God, and he said that we do not question his ways, so I was left just to wonder. So does this make us say, "Okay, what's the use? What is it really all about? Am I doing all this healthy stuff in vain, or should I keep on going and doing what's right for my body like run, swim, hike, or bike? Should I just live and eat anything and everything and hope for the best?" Coming from someone who loves to workout, I'd say keep on trucking. Keep those abs looking good and that six-pack in. Everyone has a destiny to roll on until one gets there. That's my personal opinion. Life is short and so beautiful, and all these things if you keep at them will make your body beautiful and healthy, so why not? There was a time when I took care of a gentleman who had no legs, but he still was motivated to get up each morning and tell me he had to get his early morning run in, and I'd look at him and think, "But you don't have legs." He taught me something that day. And that was you really didn't need legs to run, and he didn't literally mean run. He meant to get his body running, get it moving in spite of not having any legs. As long as he could sit up and use his arms and the rest of his body, he could work out; and in his mind, he probably did feel as if he were running once the rest of his body got going. And coming from someone who loves working out, I remember looking at him and getting discouraged because I thought when I first met him, the ad said he needed someone who could keep up with him because he's very athletic and a runner. When I saw him, I became quite upset. I had my mind set already to be active, and here he was with no legs. *How dare he misrepresent the ad he took out?* I thought. But that day, he taught me something, and that was just because one had no legs, that didn't mean he couldn't run. Life goes on. It's a lesson I'll take on through my journey while I'm still here.

A Place Called Home

So while running my adult family home, I had to learn on a daily basis what it was like to devote 90 percent of my time to these elderly folks. Is this something I really wanted to do? Why did I want to work day in and day out, changing soiled undergarments, cooking, cleaning, doing laundry, feeding, lifting, and risking back injuries? Why did I want to be around all these old folks all day long? And I would always come back with the same answer, and that was someday I would be old and that I really believed that you've got to set yourself up early by assisting our elderly. I may need it myself one day. I would always sit and look at them sometimes and wonder how they felt not being able to go to the bathroom by themselves anymore, how they felt about all these different people looking at their bodies in the nude. I remember having at least one person tell me that she didn't like other people looking at her nude body. And I tried to assure her that I would be the only one bathing her and helping with getting her clothing off and on, so she wouldn't have that worry. I quickly put myself in her place, and I thought, *Yuck, I'd really hate having different people looking at me naked.* I don't think I could do it. But if I had no choice and couldn't do it myself, I guess I'd just have to shut my eyes and get over it. Sometimes there are even male caregivers, and I could fully understand a female not wanting a male to see her body. I always tried to match the males with male and females with female. I can remember having a male caregiver get very upset because he couldn't undress and bathe the female residents. I just could not believe he argued that. It surely made me wonder what was on his mind. Although he didn't get his way, he was asked not to return to a Place Called Home. The nerve. I always thought I'd see him on the news one day for sexual assault on the elderly, but I never did. But my heart said, "Get rid of him quickly." And the female and male residents thanked me. Although the caregivers passed background checks, that doesn't mean they are not abusive; they may just have never gotten caught yet. It is so important to screen these caregivers thoroughly. After all, do we really know a person just because they appear to be nice and have a great smile and do great work? It has been my experience that these things really don't say much. And someone's integrity has to be tested over time. That's the only true way of getting a prize caregiver. Caregiving is very hard work. There are a lot of backaches, foot aches, headaches, and tiredness that come with this job. But for me, at the end of the day, when I look at these folks in their golden years, I sit back and wonder who they were and how they perform at their jobs. A lot of them had high-ranking positions. And when they got to my place, they still thought they were in those positions. I had a high-ranking military man at my place at one time, and he used to always say to me, "Soldier, how's it going today? Are we prepared for our mission this week?" At first I just tell him he wasn't in the military anymore. This went on for a couple of weeks. And then one day I thought, in this man's mind, this is where he is at this time. Why not help him be there if that's what he wants? I did the next time he called me soldier. I answered him as if I were one of his soldiers, and his eyes lit up, and his smile came back. Wow, he was just glowing with happiness. I think that that last year of his life was the best. I played soldier with him, and he got peace with this thing called Alzheimer's. And I also got him to cooperate with me in doing anything I asked in keeping the house rules. He was in charge of his platoon, and I was in charge of my home. What a wonderful time we had. So long, soldier, so long. His war had to come to an end. But in his end, he may have lost the war, but he had plenty of fight.

Chapter 3

A Place Called Home: Deciding to Close

After running a Place Called Home for a couple of years and coming up against challenges that required at least three caregivers, I decided it was time to close down. I thought it would be better working for others; at least after eight hours, I could go home and leave it all behind. It would be hard for me to work for others, especially when I was used to being the boss. I now had to accept a lower pay. One thing that I knew in this business was most owners really tried to get over on their caregivers. The excuse was they couldn't really afford to pay much. They didn't know that I knew what their monthly income was, having been an owner myself, and they could afford to pay more than minimum wage. There was so much greed going on in this business, and that's why I promised myself that I would be fair where pay was concerned or do it myself. This is hard work; and caregivers that worked hard should be paid equally for their hard work, long hours, and very challenging duties. A lot of caregivers walked off the job. Many left without any notice, and sometimes I didn't blame them, especially if they were hardworking. They only got stuck with an owner who was greedy. These kinds of situations were very bad for the residents. They'd get someone who really cared about them but then had to leave simply because their boss wasn't fair with the pay. I always said pay people enough, so they can pay their bills. What's the use of coming if you're not getting paid fairly, especially if you have children? They wanted to work the caregiver all day, and then when payday came along, the caregivers were left in shock at what they earned for many long hard hours of work. Some of the owners even pinched the food, so they didn't have a big grocery bill or kept the heat so low that the caregivers were freezing, and they were constantly moving around. All these were for the sake of taking more cash home. So I still decided to close down in spite of all the drama I'd have to put up with, working for other owners. I still know that my home was one of the best around. It was very hard to make the decision to close. My residents were very upset when I gave them the news. They gave me a piece of their minds. But I could understand their frustration. After all, they had been with me for quite some time and now have to start over and find a decent home to go to, but I did make it my duty to ensure they went to a very good home and not just anywhere. I even had the mayor call me to say what a good job I was doing and to keep up the good work. Little did he know I was getting ready to close. And that really mixed it up for me. The mayor called me. *Gosh, I better stay open*, I thought; but in the end, I decided it was time to move on. Things were starting to affect my health from taking care of everyone except Brenda. My weight was taking a serious nosedive, and sleep was something I rarely knew. It was almost like giving away my children; it was very hard. This was my passion. But I also knew that we were becoming hermits in this home. Residents didn't want anyone touching them, and no one was good enough to do the care for them but me. So it was time to go but very sadly. I thoroughly enjoyed caring for these folks and had many, many regrets about closing down after a couple of months had gone by. This is what burnout will cause you to do—make some real bad decisions because you're so tired. Your body becomes overwhelmed with exhaustion. So after getting a very long rest and doing a little traveling, I decided to get back into it; but only this time, I would be working for others. If I ever got the desire again, I could always go back one day and open up again. After working at numerous different homes, a lot of them private, which was very good, better than working in an adult family home, and witnessing abuse and disrespect in some homes, over all poor care these folks received, I became more and more anxious about reopening again. It so hurt my heart how some of these folks in their golden years didn't get gold treatment. It was clearly becoming a numbers game, and those numbers for real were about the cash! I don't want to point my finger at anyone, but the fact of the matter was there just were some bad homes. But there were plenty of great ones too. I worked in several that really were concerned about these folks, and most of them had been there from the start and had made a name for themselves. A lot of times, it's the caregiver also who may make or break a good home. So there are wrongs on both sides of the plate but more on one than the other.

The Search for a Regular Job

Well, pretty much after I closed my place, I got plenty of rest and decided to start with the job search again; and since I was briefly living in Atlanta, I thought what better place to look for this type of work. I was sure people, pay, everything would be different because I was in another state. One of my first clients to care for in Atlanta was Katie. This lady had Alzheimer's and was pretty much very pleasant to work for. Most days were spent going to the mall, to the park, etc. Before I got there, I think basically this lady went nowhere. But at home with her daughter, who was a chef, Katie held a normal conversation, so I would say she had a light case of Alzheimer's. I say this because she was very cooperative and was acting very normally. She seemed to be a bit unusual for someone with this disease. Some days her family would take her out to dinner, but besides that, she didn't get out too much although I welcomed the opportunity to care for one person. It was nothing like being my own boss. The relief of caring for six people and seeing all the death and dying was a great break for me too. I'd like to talk a little about taking on more than you should and getting burned out. You should always have backup and at least two permanently employed caregivers on staff. Doing what I did should never be done, although I did it and tried to be the super caregiver. I became a very tired and grouchy person. I wasn't eating properly or really caring for my own self at all. These folks had become my children almost. In the end, we all became very attached. I didn't want anyone touching them, and they didn't want anyone touching them unless it was me. We had a couple of bad caregivers in there also whom I fired, so this was a big deciding factor in doing it myself. In the beginning, it was great just us, no other caregiver to follow behind, to make sure the care was being done like I wanted it to (properly). But about six months in, I became very tired, but I couldn't let my folks down. I had to keep going for them. Quickly into a year and a few other issues that occurred, I thought, yes, it's my health or the care home. So it was time to go. By never trying to take care of six by yourself, it'll only work for a short time. It's a very serious deal. I once had a friend who was very overweight, who had two homes running, one in which she worked a shift, but she also had plenty of health issues bothering her. But she would not give up being in the home and leave her qualified caregivers to do the care. Forgive me for this statement. There was a lot of greed going on in her head. Well, to make a long story short, because she ignored her health and put greed at the top of her list, she is no longer here with us. You've gotta take care of yourself, especially if you're gonna be in an ownership position. Caregiving is a tough job. But it has its rewards if you can look at the reward as a service to help someone, a reward with lots of integrity and not a monetary reward. Speaking for myself, the feeling I get is just unexplainable. It's what I do. While you are reading the pages of my book, and you're thinking about doing this type of work, or you're simply a daughter or son whose parent was stricken with this horrid disease, I hope that it will give you lots of help and insight as to what decisions to make for your loved one. Please do a favor for me, if I can be so bold to ask. When you make your decisions, please take your time, please.

Auntie, He Cannot Stay

This is a story about my dear sweet aunt who is no longer with us anymore. But I felt the need to include her in my book. My dear auntie lost her husband to this awful disease. I remember visiting the both of them when they both were alive. I was also running my care home in another town. As we sat and talked, I remember talking to him, and the language of Alzheimer's as I call it started to speak coming from my uncle's mouth. I say the language of Alzheimer's because they have their own vocabulary that only few can understand, and I feel privileged to be one of the few. Auntie asked me,

"Brenda, he's gonna get better, isn't he?" I hesitated for a couple of minutes and said, "Auntie, no, he won't." I then asked her if anyone had informed her or met with her to tell her about the process of Alzheimer's, and she quickly said no. I was bothered about this because no one in the medical field had informed her on what would happen to her husband as the disease progressed. She didn't know what to expect. All this time, she thought that he would be getting better and spending the rest of his days with her. I felt so sad for her. I could see the expression change on her face, the sadness in her eyes—she really had no words after that. I took it upon myself to lightly explain to her what changes would come so that she would be more informed and know what was happening when he came out of the room with three shirts on or two pairs of pants instead of constantly telling him over and over, words that he could never understand. I always from that day wished I had my home in that town so that maybe I could somehow make her days and nights a little easier, giving her comfort by being there for her with answers if she would have questions about the disease. I did tell her that Alzheimer's is an irreversible brain failure, and the process can take years before it's noticeable. Alzheimer's robs the individual of their mind. No one plans to get Alzheimer's; it's just something that unexpectedly comes on. After getting Alzheimer's, a person usually lives about eight years, sometimes longer. After the age of sixty-five, your chances of getting Alzheimer's increase. By seventy-five, you have a 10 percent chance. Alzheimer's is very scary for most of the population. Those that are family members of the ones who have it wonder if they will get it too. More often than not, some other children in the family will get it. Then sometimes no one else will.

Sharing Space in Your Home

If you have to care for a relative that has Alzheimer's in your home, before taking them in, consider a couple of things: how well do you get along with them? That person that you remember and the person that they have become may or may not be a fit for you. You may have gotten along with them well when he or she was normal. But people who have Alzheimer's change and forget and have little or no memory of who you are. This will also affect your living situation with them. They may become combative; they may be very withdrawn from you, and if they have or get sundowners, there will be a lot of nights when you will be up. You may be spending almost all your time attending to them and sometimes forgetting your own needs. This will get old very quickly and lead to burnout. Sometimes when you're burned out, you will become angry and grouchy, and a lot of days you will feel like not even assisting them when you know that they cannot help themselves and the care becomes too much for you and you want your life back. This is time for you to seriously find care elsewhere; at this point, your help will really not be the kind of help they need. If you're used to having your bedroom door open and unlocked, this will have to change. They will start to wander in there and start taking your things, and you probably won't find them for weeks to months, and this alone can be upsetting. You will have to lock up things that are special to you. As I mentioned before, when things go missing, they're gone. It is so fascinating how they can hide things. And don't count on them helping to find them; they will have no idea what you are talking about. You'll just have to wait to run into it one day when you're looking for something else. As far as they're concerned, everything in your home is now theirs; and as far as they know, this may be their home. If you don't have strong patience and great understanding of their disease, if you can tell yourself that this is the disease and not the real person, then each time there is a crisis, you'll be okay; but if you're the type who has a short supply of patience, then find the best care home that you can and take them there. As the sole caregiver, you will experience loneliness, sometimes tears, tiredness, regret, burnout, and eagerness; at some point, you want to just run away. So please consider, if you have another relative or friend who may be willing to share the care load, then bring them along. In the end, you'll be very thankful that you did. Doing it alone will not make you last long and will leave you tired, angry, and bitter. You don't want that. You'll know in your heart that is not what you really feel, but that is what it will get to at some point. You've gotta get a break sometime, or you don't even need to go there in the first place.

He's Not the Man He Was

When hiring people to come to your home as your caregiver through an agency, word of mouth, private, whatever the situation, you'll discover that sometimes the person you are to care for can be belligerent. They often hate change and can sometimes notice it and decide to act out. You will become offended and want to leave. Well, you should always be informed to not take this personally. Now that I've worked with almost every kind of disability out there, I want to talk about a situation that I took personally, but I still maintained the professional that I am. I was faced with racism. Now from what I was told, this person would have never been that way before they got Alzheimer's. I was constantly called black, the n word, and so on. I found that in most folks with Alzheimer's, it's amazing how they can forget a name, a face, or a place, except for words that are related to slander and racism. They can be very insulting about a person's weight also. And if you are a professional or someone that responded to an ad, you absolutely cannot take insults personally. You have to dig down inside and let it go unless they're getting physical. Then you should leave and find another type of profession. They won't change. It's a losing battle to try to talk to them about it or tell them to stop. What I always did with this particular person was redirect him, get him quickly involved in something else, or quickly start talking about something else. One thing I found was they won't win the speaking race. Most people with Alzheimer's cannot talk at very fast paces, and I have that gift of gab, so I was a lot faster. In this situation, redirecting always worked; and after a while, they quit altogether. You have to be very clever and witty sometimes. I've seen people cry and really take some insults very personally and quit the job even when they were warned of the person's personality before taking the job. I had people tell me, "Oh, they need to make them stop talking like that." And I'd tell them, "Before you continue to care for people who have Alzheimer's, you need to take a short course on caring for them or go to the library and check out books on it." You will not get anywhere making suggestions such as these, so don't waste your time. Rather, go and get educated about it first before you decide on becoming a caregiver. Don't just take this type of work simply because you need an income coming in. You'll soon see that it's not for you, and you will end up looking for work elsewhere. It is not the type of job that you'd take very lightly. These folks are truly depending on you for their daily living activities, so if it's not in you, don't get involved.

She Saw a Man Sitting on Her Bed

Some people with Alzheimer's have hallucinations and sometimes see things or people who have been deceased for years. I had a little lady who would constantly run from her room, claiming to have seen a man sitting on her bed or simply someone she didn't know. She'd do this a couple times per week. It got to the point that I wondered if there really was someone there or not. I can remember one night that she was so afraid that she ran and jumped in the bed with me, and I could feel her shaking. This was like a small child having nightmares and jumping in the bed with Mommy, only this time it was a grown-up with Alzheimer's. I had to resolve her dilemma somehow, so I decided to move her to another room, and that took care of her situation after a while. As I discussed this with her doctor, he informed me that 40 percent of people with Alzheimer's have psychosis over the course of their illness, which is really a mental illness. This is why she was constantly seeing these people who really were not there. But since it was my first time experiencing that kind of behavior, out of all the people I had taken care of, it somewhat frightened me. After researching and speaking with other adult care home owners, I found that several of them had residents that did the same thing too. So this made me feel a little better. I still question whether or not this was hallucination or not. Anyway, that's for another book. I can remember the other residents watching as she came speeding out of her room; they wondered what was up with her. Some would look as though they were afraid, and some would laugh. I mean really, really laugh. There was a time when she ran under the dining room table just like a two-year-old would when playing hide-and-seek or something. The experiences I got from caring for these folks were unreal at times. So many of them act exactly alike by doing the same things, and then there are a few that act nothing like the others. Most of them do the clothing thing—you know, piling on clothing. They do the sundowners thing up at night, the hoarding thing, and forgetting thing. But out of the twenty-five years of working with these folks, I can say I've met at least two or more that have done things totally different. Usually if you ask a person with Alzheimer's to count from one to ten, they can't. But I've met a lady with midstages of Alzheimer's who could count to ten easily and was going further until I stopped her. But she did have a few of the actions others with this disease had, like hiding and taking things that didn't belong to her or sundowning. But that was about it. This was so strange to me. If she was just diagnosed, I could understand it more, but she had this disease for a few years. And usually by this time, you don't really know anything much or anyone. She could also hold a conversation almost normally, but as it went on, you could see that her words didn't add up or make sense. But just the fact that she held a conversation for so long and steadily was puzzling. I think I could pretty much talk anyone under the table, but this lady got my tongue tied. I mean she really did. I looked into it again the following day to find out if someone may have misdiagnosed her. But no, I was told she had Alzheimer's. I guess maybe she was just strong-willed and refused to let this disease slow her down for as long as she could, and I say amen to that.

She Doesn't Dress the Same Anymore

It becomes very baffling at times for family members when they see their family member with this disease change right before their eyes. Someone who may have been a sharp dresser, very stylish, may come out of the bedroom with something you yourself know they wouldn't be caught dead in. In this case, their long-term memory overrides their short-term memory; she may remember that she had to put on clothing but never remembered that she used to be a very stylish dresser. And most times they'll forget to even change clothing altogether. I can remember having a lady at one time who totally forgot to dress. She came out her room with only her necklace, purse, and shoes. She even put on a pair of earrings. The funny thing about it all was the shoes, necklace, purse, and earrings were all red. She had at one time been a stylish dresser. I think in her case she could remember to try to match up her clothing. She put on only the little accessories to go with her outfit but forgot the outfit altogether. Thank god, I was there with her family when this happened. If they hadn't laughed, I would have only laughed in my mind. It's always good to go through their closets and take out all those fancy things and retire them but always save a couple of nice outfits for a night out with their family or for the holidays. But other than that, plan on wash and wear from then on. I liked to keep their hair fixed if they were the type who had their hair styled nicely all the time, and I made sure that if they were going out to a special dinner with family or some event. If they used to be a snappy dresser, I tried to always dress them close to the nines. For all of you who don't know what that old term means, let me get more modern: they'd be the bomb! Family members always appreciated it. Just because they have Alzheimer's didn't mean to me that they had to look like someone who was ill. I've taken ladies out with me and really dolled them up. And unless someone tried to hold a conversation with them, you'd really think they were a business lady or just a well-dressed woman. I pretty much dressed them how I would want to be dressed if I was going out to a special place or strolling through the mall. And I'm sure that if those ladies could remember that they were sharp dressers, and even though they had Alzheimer's, someone took the time to keep them looking marvelous, they'd be so grateful. I know I would. I always hated to see the ones who could be dressed decently if anything just lying around in a gown or sweats all day. Although it's mostly wash and wear, that didn't mean that wash and wear couldn't be nuzzled up a little. Oh yes, it can be done. My dear sweet mother is no longer here with me; she wasn't the sharp dresser, but she was a neat and very clean dresser. And if I had the opportunity to dress her when she couldn't do it herself, I'd sure make sure she was dressed how I always remembered her. I'm sure you'd want this for your mom too. I guess if I could dress every person with Alzheimer's and make them resemble their old selves, then when they looked in the mirror, at least they may remember who they are. Wouldn't that be great? To all of you out there who has taken the time to read my book, if you have a mom or dad living at home with you, and they are not very combative or busy, please take the time to keep them looking just like dear old dad or mom always did. If you let them look in the mirror, they may just happen to catch a glimpse of someone they once knew. Try it yourself. You may be surprised.

Denial

A lot of family members would like to keep their family member at home because there is a lot of bad news floating around out there about nursing homes, care homes, etc. If I may only give my opinion, I'd say it depended on how calm and laid-back your loved one is. If they are a busybody, then are you prepared to stay home with them 24/7 to cook, clean, bathe, the whole nine yards? People with Alzheimer's go through changes. They seem to go from one step to another, getting worse and worse all the time. Now in the beginning of the diagnosis, you may be able to handle them. You may even be able to hold a pretty decent conversation with them, but as the disease progresses, they may become uncontrollable. They may have you up at night; they may become combative. Are you able to pay a caregiver to come in to help with the care? You have to almost look at this as bringing a new baby home from the hospital. You have to lock things up, put things away. You basically eventually have to childproof the home as the disease gets worse. Now they may turn out to be calm through the entire illness if you're so lucky. But most of my experiences showed me busybodies, in the end, who gave me a run for my money. I've even seen family members in tears not only from exhaustion but also from a lot of things. They hate to see their loved one in that condition. They are in disbelief. Some even think that one morning they will wake up, and their loved one would have slept this disease off, and all is better now. Let me tell ya, total denial. It ain't gonna be that way. I've known of wives hating to put their husbands in a home because they themselves are fearful of being alone, probably in the twenty to forty years of marriage and living with that person at home all those years. All of a sudden, their loved one may have to leave home. So they get into strong denial, thinking that they are stronger than the Alzheimer's and can keep their loved one at home with them. Then after months of doing it alone, they find themselves burned out, angry, tired, sad, and mad at the world for what has happened to their life partner. As I stated a few chapters back, this is a hard job, and it needs a lot of careful thought and maybe even some counseling before you try to care for your loved one at home. Sometimes you just have to let go no matter how heartbreaking it may be for you. It will be for the best. Believe me. When it gets like that—you're angry, tired, and sad—it's time to stop! You'll only end up treating them badly from all the exhaustion you're feeling. So with all this said, find a great care home. Visit them as much as possible and give them lots of hugs and kisses when you see them. We all hate to see our loved ones down, sick, and hurt. We can't control or do anything about it or stop what's happened to them. But bringing exhaustion to yourself, behind it, surely will not help them at all! Figuring out the best plan of care for them would be the best solution. Letting go is always hard, but know in the case of Alzheimer's, you will only be hurting yourself by trying to hold on to and having a love relationship with that person; this will be impossible. Now don't get me wrong. I said love relationship, not being-in-love relationship. You can always be in love with them and hold love in your heart always. But the person that you always knew will become a bright light that will slowly fade away. So be there for as long as that light shines bright. Then when it finally goes out, be ready to walk away from the darkness and continue to hold them forever in your heart. You'll always have great loving memories, and nothing can ever take that away from you.

Taking Care of Yourself

I can remember when I was taking care of six people all alone. The first six months were a piece of cake; then I noticed I was slowly becoming grouchy, not wanting to get up out of bed on some mornings. But being the people pleaser that I am, the show had to go on. I just couldn't let my people down, even though on most mornings I just wanted to run away. You have got to take care of yourself first before taking care of someone with Alzheimer's. You must make sure you are in good health. Sometimes we caregivers are so caught up in caring for the person needing care that we forget ourselves. Kinda like a wife after having children; they forget themselves and even the husband, leaving him jealous because he was no longer getting the attention like the one before the kids came. It's somewhat the same thing with caring for these folks. But always take care of yourself first. There is no possible way you can take care of a person with Alzheimer's if you yourself have poor health. You will quickly find out that you cannot keep up with them, especially if they're a busybody. What saved me was the fact that I have always worked out, and around the time I started in this field, I was already in good physical shape and very strong; and for a while, I continued to work out for as long as I could. But soon the load became too heavy. I was alone caring for these folks, and most of them were very busy. Sleep became a luxury for me instead of a necessity. Some days I got by on only three hours of sleep. Wooh! Looking back, I just don't know how I did it. I can remember getting up, helping all six of the residents, and feeling like I could faint at any time. There was a day when I got these red bumps breaking out all over my arms and the sides of my rib area. Eventually, I went to the doctor who told me that this was my nerves and wanted to know what I did for work. Once I talked this over with him, his diagnosis was that the bumps on my skin were my nerves. I was very overworked and under tremendous stress. And the only advice he could give me, along with a prescription for prednisone, was to get help caring for these folks or become a resident in bed myself. Well, I can tell you that that really scared me and left a lot of room for thought as far as getting help went. So with that said, all you caregivers out there, you've just gotta get help caring for your loved one. The stress alone will almost take your health, if not kill you. Trying to be superwoman or—man won't get it. I even went from a perfect size 10 down to a size 4 or 5 in no time. Now some of you may think that a size 5 is a great size to be. Yes, it is—if you're five feet tall—and I was not that short. I sometimes resembled a walking skeleton. But putting weight on and off was always easy for me. I could always lose when I wanted to and put it back when I thought I needed it. It's just that at that time I was so busy caring for all these other folks that I completely forgot myself. I wanted to make sure that all the children were okay. I was always a chronic people pleaser. But it won't hurt to put yourself first if you're a people pleaser like me.

Abused and Mistreated

I've always taken a stand toward elderly care facilities and those caring for our elderly. I tell you this story because it really affected me mentally and professionally. And the person it happened to didn't have to endure the sufferings she suffered. This is also why when you are seeking a care facility, you should go looking with your eyes wide open and investigate the facility you choose very thoroughly. My heart went out to the family members of this little lady whom I will call Sara. Sara was a little lady who weighed about ninety pounds and was approximately five feet tall. When I went to work at this private care home, I was somewhat impressed with the layout of the home; it was fairly clean and modern. I noticed right away that Sara was very hyper and busy, constantly moving around the home, but I also noticed that she had feces on her skin. Having to ask the staff myself what her care needs were, I was told that she had a condition where her colon was exposed to the outside of her body (gastroschisis). She needed to have continuous care and cleaning and monitoring at all times, although that was not the situation with these caregivers. Sara was basically ignored most of the time because of her condition. Even though these caregivers were there to assist this lady, they'd rather watch television. I quickly became attached to Sara. I thought she was very cute, and right away, the owner assigned me to care for her. I noticed that the owner didn't really care for Sara and was always talking down to her. I wondered why she took this lady into her home when she didn't seem to care for her but looked at her with disgust. Even though Sara had this condition, I still felt close to her, and I knew I was there to care for her and not to judge her like the rest of the staff seemed to be doing. As I came into work one morning, I found

Sara had been beaten with black eyes and bruises everywhere. The owner's only excuse was she fell. But I knew better. The owner's daughter, a bold and bully-type nineteen-year-old, took it upon herself to tell me how Sara made her sick and how she had a part in the condition I found Sara in that morning. I didn't know why she thought that I would keep her secret. I quickly reported this abuse to Sara's family members and the state for an investigation, which led to the closing of the care home and the conviction of the owner and her daughter. Sara was moved to a better facility after recuperating from her wounds, and I was thanked by family members, which made me feel very good. But I was harassed for a couple of weeks by members of the owner's family until police put a stop to them also. Please be careful where you place your loved one. Be so thorough in your search for a creditable care facility or private home. Sara's family members paid good money, expecting quality care for their loved one, but was only tricked because of greed. They took this lady in and neglected her needs. My heart went out to Sara. I'm sure that she suffered a lot of abuse before I came along, and I really to this day believe that God placed me in that home because he knew I would tell someone about the treatment of Sara. No one else seemed to even care. This goes on in plenty of care homes throughout the United States. Some are found out while others are never exposed. But by selecting quality-care people, getting quality references and background checks, we can at least slow down or stop bad treatment of our elderly.

Once an Adult, Twice a Child

And if you can get personal references on your caregivers and ones with great experience, it may save you a lot of heartache.

A Tribute to Those Who Lost to Alzheimer's

Charles Bronson (actor)—thanks for all the great movies. I enjoyed them so.

Winston Churchill (prime minister of Great Britain, a place I one day hope to see)

Perry Como (singer)—thanks for all the beautiful songs, especially for Christmas.

Aaron Copeland (composer)—thanks for the joyful sounds.

Willem de Kooning (artist)—thanks for giving us vision through your eyes.

Ralph Waldo Emerson (writer)—thanks for the giving me inspiration.

Barry Goldwater (U.S. senator from Arizona)—thanks for being you.

William Hanna (animator, Hanna-Barbera)—thanks for all the great toys and cartoon shows.

Charlton Heston (actor)—thanks for the great movies, like *The Ten Commandments*.

Queen Juliana Wilhelmina (queen of the Netherlands)—hope it was good to be.

Beatrice Little (comedian)—thanks for making us laugh!

Jack Lord (actor)—thanks for entertaining my mom in her favorite *Hawaii Five-O.*

Burgess Meredith (actor)—your show gave me dreams.

Iris Murdoch (novelist and philosopher)—thanks for giving people like me inspiration.

Maurice Ravel (composer)—thanks for being giving to us.

Ronald Reagan (U.S. president)—thanks for leading us. Your presence is in my stories.

Sugar Ray Robinson (boxer)—thanks for knocking them out till the end. You gave lots of men hope.

Norman Rockwell (artist)—I love your pictures and novelty items.

May you rest in peace.

Chapter 4

Stories of Past Clients

Back in the mid-1980s, I worked in the area called Brighton Beach. This was in New York City. There was a little lady whom I shall call Ann. When I went to Ann, I was told that she had Alzheimer's disease. After being there for about six months, I clearly saw that Ann probably had more of a mental illness than anything else. I would come into work, and Ann would hide things from me. I'd take the ingredients out to prepare dinner, and they would disappear, never to be found again. This went on for quite some time until I got smart and set up a plan where Ann could no longer do this. Sometimes when I got ready to go home, my coat would disappear. So to remedy that, I started leaving my coat in a gym bag I started bringing. One day, we were on our way to the bank. I always let Ann carry her check in her own purse. On this day, upon getting to the bank, I asked Ann to take the check out to be deposited into her account, but the check all of a sudden disappeared. It was so baffling to me because I secured the check into her purse myself.

Well, wouldn't you know, the check couldn't be found anywhere. So with great embarrassment, we had to leave the bank with no business transaction that day. Ann was very clever. As soon as we returned to the house, she quickly pulled the check from the purse. I thought, *Is she a magician or what?* She had the check. I decided to leave that issue to her son from then on. My duties were to cook, clean, and run errands for Ann as needed. And this was because she supposedly had Alzheimer's, so I was told in the beginning. On one quiet sunny day, I decided to do some spring cleaning and hang some curtains for Ann while she relaxed in the living room. The curtains were really looking great, so I continued with my work. All of a sudden, I felt a sharp aching pain run through my shoulder. It was so painful that I barely got myself down off the step ladder. I knew that someone had stabbed me, but I had no idea that it was Anna. Out of nowhere, Anna decided she wanted to stab me for no apparent reason. She just felt like doing it, she said. After attending to my wound, I called her son. My injury now was feeling like a really bad toothache and was throbbing really bad. I probably should have been on my way to the hospital, but I thought it would be okay. Her son finally showed up and was very upset with his mother. I questioned him about whether or not she really had Alzheimer's. I really thought at this point she had been wrongly diagnosed, or I hadn't been told the truth. I told her son how the day went and that I probably wouldn't be back, especially after being stabbed in the shoulder. I'm glad it was my shoulder and not my face or chest area. I knew now that this lady was mentally ill. After speaking with her son the next day, I decided to give him one more chance. She continued to hide and steal things and refuse personal hygiene, and she was very combative about it. This went on for about three more weeks until I decided I had enough, and it was time to move on. I was never told the truth about Ann's real condition. But at this point, I didn't even care. Be very careful when you're going out to work for others, and this is for all the caregivers out there looking for work. We always go to the client for an interview, but from experience, I've learned that you must always conduct an interview yourself. Interview who you will possibly be working for. They may not be a good fit for you. Always try to see if the client can provide proof from their family that their diagnosis is really Alzheimer's or whatever they say it is. You do not want to get fooled into thinking your client has one disease, and you find it's something else. This could save you time and injuries. Better safe than sorry!

Poor Choices on the Menu

Ahhh, poor choices on the menu. There was a home with unbelievable meal choices. I couldn't really believe that someone could be so coldhearted and feed a human being some of the food items they chose and still call them dinner. The owner of this home only kept females. When I first set foot in her home, I said, "Oh, this is homey and cute, quiet, and clean." Like in most care homes, my duties were to cook, clean, and maintain good hygiene for these clients, assist in medication, etc. Since my shift was from 10:00 a.m. to 6:00 p.m., I was responsible for preparing dinner while the owner went out for her evening meal. Since there were only three ladies in this home, I thought dinner would be easy. But I always tried to make sure that the dinner was special and memorable. After all, this was about all they had to look forward to, day in and day out. So I decided on meatloaf, mashed potatoes, broccoli, carrots, and apple pie and ice cream for dessert. These foods were soft and would be easy for these ladies to chew and swallow. As I prepared the dinner, I always had the residents come into the kitchen to watch; and if someone could assist, I'd let them. This was to make them feel at home, and sometimes they may feel they were at their old residence. Just as we got everything on going and cooking, the owner came back in. Something smelled good until she saw what I was cooking. I could not believe my ears. She hit the roof! "Are you nuts?" she said. "What is this? Why are you giving them meat loaf and potatoes? I don't give them that fancy food. I can't afford it." So I responded, "Well, why is it here then? This is a good dinner for them." She quickly told me that I didn't pay for the food there. At that point, I just got quiet. She was so upset she took the meat loaf and threw it in the garbage, along with the rest. It was a perfectly great meat loaf. I just couldn't believe it. I asked if there was something else she wanted me to cook, and her response was yes, breathing heavily. "I'll show you." She then took out four cans of Vienna sausages, four Snickers bars, some instant breakfast drink mix, and milk. She blended it to a soup-like texture, warmed it up, and gave it to these ladies together with crackers. She then said, "They like this." What hurt me so bad was these poor ladies had been getting this every day and were afraid to speak up for themselves. I just figured this lady has to be mentally ill, and she must be reported. The owner even attempted to show me how to mix this for them each day. I asked her how she would like to eat that every day; her response was "I can eat it. See, it tastes good." I managed to whisper to the ladies that I would get them help and that they wouldn't be eating that crap any longer and that I would have the state there first thing the next day. I finished my day and left, telling the owner I would see her the next day with no intentions of ever coming back. The state did come and question the ladies, and the home was closed down. This poor menu choice was all for the sake of greed. Some people just have no respect for their sisters or brothers in Christ.

Taking Care of a Little Rascal

One summer I was asked to care for a man I will call Ben Matters. I was told he was one of the last living Little Rascals, you know, from the show *The Little Rascals*. He had quite a lot of evidence around his home that would say he was one of the last original ones. We went to McDonald's every Thursday morning for breakfast. This man was fascinated with the breakfast burrito they served. One thing I didn't quite like about him was on our way out of the restaurant, he'd stuff his bag with paper napkins, creamer, spoons, forks, sugars, salt—whatever they had out on the counter that was free. Most times I would be so embarrassed I'd walk far in front of him. Although people came up to him for his autograph, he still didn't seem to get embarrassed about his little habit. And then came time to get into my car. At that time, I drove a small little car, and Ben was over three hundred pounds. So the car always went down on his side, plus he smoked worse than a choo-choo train—and in my car. I should have told him that he couldn't smoke in there, but I never did. So there we went driving down the street in a smoke-filled car. Oh, I was so very sick of it. You see, Ben didn't really care too much about his health, and since he was a child star, you'd think he would be. But nope, he really couldn't care less about his own health. He'd light up a nonmenthol cigarette; and when it was down to the butt or filter, he'd take that and then light up another, only this one had to be regular flavor. Besides being a diabetic, Mr. Matters was a semi-hoarder. By looking in his closet, you could surely tell that he had spent some time in McDonald's: he had just about every toy that came out since the place opened. He always told me that they would be worth something one day. And he may be right! He'd sit and tell me stories of long ago, when he was acting on the show *The Little Rascals.* He even gave me some autographed photos of him and *The Little Rascals* gang. Mr. Matters was a heavy-set man and did not respect his diabetes one bit. This was probably why his toes were always being amputated. But that didn't seem to worry him one bit as long as he could keep being a chain-smoker and eating about ten Snickers bars per day. He sure could put away the sweets. Now Mr. Matters didn't have Alzheimer's or dementia. He was just an elderly man needing help, mostly with his diabetes and house work. People in the area seem to like him and were always asking for his autograph, people around his age that remembered who and what *The Little Rascals* show was. I surely remembered and watched it as a child. Despite suffocating in the cigarette smoke all the time, I really enjoyed being around Mr. Matters. He was a nice man, just demanding when it came to his cigarettes. If he ran out of cigarettes, he would try to run me all over town just to find his brand; and this I didn't like, especially when he didn't offer any gas money. Oh yeah! He was a cheap man too! Eventually, the smoke and demanding ways finally got to me. I quit one day because he really got upset that I wouldn't drive out to the air force base to buy his cigarettes since they were cheaper out there. He threw a tantrum just like a child while not offering any gas money for this long drive. I was not in the air force, so they weren't going to let me on post anyway. But you couldn't get that through his head. At that point, I thought it was time to go. One thing I really didn't expect was disrespect.

After a few years went by, I got married and had a new baby girl. I always wondered what happened to Mr. Matters, so I decided to visit him and introduce him to my little girl. But when I arrived, I was told he had died. We departed on a sour note. But I still really did enjoy the wisdom I got from him. May he rest in peace. So long, friend.

Pets in the Care Home

Having pets in the care home can be good and therapeutic for residents, but it could also turn into a tragedy. This is why I will tell you about a home. I happened to be employed at one that had fully grown dogs running freely through the home, and when I say fully grown, I'm talking about horse size. This is an awful idea, I thought, when I informed the owner. You have people walking around with walkers, and some cannot hear or see well. In this owner's opinion, the residents would go before her untrained and unruly mutts. These dogs ran through the home knocking down furniture; one even slammed into me as I prepared the evening dinner. As I constantly complained to the owner that this was an accident waiting to happen, she let me know that my calls would not be heard. Merle—I will call her—was about as sweet as sugar. The owner was always on her for something, but I always found a way to talk to her and bring her comfort. I knew that there would be a day that I would have to bring these folks peace in their old age and assure them that they would no longer have to fear of being knocked down by these huge dogs running through the home. Merle was very petite and frail; she always walked slowly. On this day, the biggest dog was running for a meal and knocked poor Merle to the floor. That did it for me. Thank god, as frail as she was, other than being sore the next day, she wasn't seriously hurt at all. But the incident was reported to the family members. This home was not only packed with animals running wild, but lots of trash was always around. No matter how much you tried to keep it clean, this adult family home was just filthy. My days there were numbered, just as soon as something better came along. The state finally came in but thought the trash and filth was not a problem. I was floored with surprise. They didn't even think the dogs were a hazard. But I did see to it that Merle's family removed her from the horrible mess. I couldn't do anything about the rest of the residents since the state was responsible for them. The elderly love pets. Small little pups or even a cat is good therapy for these folks but not a big horse-size dog running rampant through a home where people are using walkers. If you pick a home for your loved one, make sure if there are animals, they are well trained and small, probably cats more than dogs. These dogs were just trouble because no one took the time to housebreak them. And because of the selfishness of the owner, she allowed them to eventually cause an accident. They also ate from the table and garbage bins inside the home. Till this day, I still cannot see why the state didn't see any of this as hazardous to these folks' health.

Sometimes the people we put in authority will also turn a blind eye.

A Nurse-run Home

This particular home was run by a so-called nurse. She hired me immediately but wanted to pay me very little, even with my experience and credentials, again moving along until the right pay and right care home came along. This is another home that was very unprofessionally set up and not so clean. These men were all veterans, and in my opinion, they served our country. We should give back by giving great care to these retired men. This nurse served peanut butter and jelly for most meals at lunch and somewhat decent meals for dinner. You'd think that she would be happy to give great care to these men and happily cook the best meal she could think of. I am sure they would have really appreciated that. She had a veteran who I will call Rodger. Rodger was a nice guy who had been hurt in the war, so this left him with no feeling from his chest all the way to his feet. He was what we called total care. Someone needed to do everything for him. After all, at the rate of $10,000 per month, he should have gotten first-class service. But most of the time, he was left alone until he soiled his pants. If you talked to Rodger, you'd quickly see that he was a very kind and soft-spoken man who loved to converse every once in a while. Rodger had a problem with swallowing, so I didn't think peanut butter and jelly was a good lunch for him. Peanut butter always sticks to the roof of your mouth. But I was told because she was a nurse and I wasn't, she knew what would be best for her resident. So I just replied, "Okay, you're the boss." Every time this man ate peanut butter and jelly, he began to choke and gag very hard and could not breathe. Almost every time he ate this for lunch, the owner would have to perform CPR on him because he'd aspirate and choke on the sandwich. He could not swallow the peanut butter. I'd always suggest getting a thickener and perhaps serving him a hot soup. It was wintertime anyway. Instead of the two of us working together to find a solution to fix this problem, she'd become angry and thought that I was trying to tell her how to do her job. Meanwhile, poor Rodger would have to suffer. This went on several more times; the menu didn't change. 911 was called many times. The last time before I decided to quit, 911 came again; but before they got there, the owner performed CPR on poor Rodger and beat his chest until I heard his ribs crack. I really wasn't convinced she knew what she was doing. Rodger did not need to be there. This home and many others like it had so much greed going on that they didn't care about these folks' feelings just as long as the money kept coming in. I don't know what happened to Rodger. But I know that I could no longer stay around and watch another scene like that again. I'm sure he probably ended up dying there. The only person that supposedly cared for him seemed to only come around to pay the owner and say hi to Rodger on her way out. So

I don't think he had relatives that cared too much for him. As for the owner, she needed to go back to nursing school because there were a lot of trainings she seemed to miss out on, and one was dressing appropriately and not walking around in house slippers and a robe all day. She showed no shame when professionals came around.

There Are Some Good Homes Out There

I don't mean to knock all the homes down because there are a lot of good homes out there. I just felt that the state was giving out too many licenses to the wrong people. At one time, they were giving licenses out to everyone and anyone. People were really abusing the system strictly for greed. The state has raised the fee to get a license and changed a few of the regulations. But that didn't stop the greed, and people opened up for the wrong reasons. I've been to many fine homes where people were treated with respect and honor. They were served very appetizing meals and good snacks. There was plenty of great activity and great caregivers. But sadly, there are more bad ones than good, and as many complaints the state received, you'd think they'd make it a little harder to get licensed than simply charging more money to be licensed. Everything seemed to be about money based on how much money someone got. I think that they should have changed it to where you'd at least have to have a nursing degree to open up one of these homes instead of a simple GED. Maybe they will in the near future. When I first started out, you didn't even need to have a GED. You didn't need a thing, just $100 and orientation and a home that would pass an inspection—very simple. People started seeing how simple this was and how much money they could potentially make, and soon they were overflooded with applications. It was like an open candy store. People basically were thinking that they hit the lottery. I know of at least three nurse-run homes that are excellently run, and I'm sure there are more. But there also are a few run by bad nurses, sad to say. If you are looking for a home, even though some that say nurse is on duty twenty-four hours, that doesn't mean you're going to get a great place for your mom or dad. I've seen a lot of people get fooled by this. They passed up great homes that didn't have a nurse running them and later were very disappointed by the choice that they made. Shop for this home as if you yourself were going to live in it. I've seen homes that looked just like mansions, and you think a king lived there. A lot of people thought, "My, these people must be eating steak and lobster every day." Not. They were barely getting the basics. The inside of the home was beautiful, and the owners had beautiful cars and beautiful furnishings that they barely wanted people to touch. But the food was a-w-f-u-l. Again, people flocked there because of the expensive decor and were sold but didn't take the time to really investigate the true goings-on inside the home. You must be thorough in your search for the right place. I feel that the smaller care facilities are far more perfect than the bigger more crowded places. There are certainly more one-on-one interactions going on than one to every five or six people. Nurse aides are overworked and underpaid and sometimes don't do as well in caring because of burnout and overload of clients to care for. So a lot of times you'll find residents just sitting alone along the corridors with no one talking to them, something I'm very sympathetic about. It makes me very sad. I can remember when the word got out about adult family homes. People immediately ran after a license, not because they were professionals looking for a great business caring for our elderly but because of greed. I had people coming to me and asking me how much I made, which really upset me. They would also ask if I could show them how to get a license. Some were even willing to do fraudulent things to get a license. That's how bad greed had struck them. It just amazed me how fast the word of the business spread and how fast it got into the wrong hands. At that time, you'd hear of lots of people getting in trouble for taking vacations and leaving the residents with incompetent caregivers. People were dying because an inexperienced caregiver gave someone the wrong medications. This was all because of greed, and it quickly turned something that was supposed to be a new kind of care situation for our elderly into something scary and not good; the gossip also spread like wildfire. This is still going on today. Hopefully, by the time my book is hot off the presses, changes in getting a license are in place. I sure hope so. Don't you?

It Could Be You

You know, we go through life thinking that we are gonna live forever. No one really wants to think they're gonna die anytime soon. We see everyone around us dying, getting sick, and being hospitalized. But we still don't think this will ever be us. This only happens to other people. But you know, I truly think that we are all in a long line, and God comes and gets you when he wants or when it's your turn in line. Now a lot of you may think that this is silly or even stupid. But if you think about it, it could be your last day on this earth after reading his book, or this could be the last page I will ever write. Hope not. Seriously, time waits for no man or woman. It's hard for me to imagine leaving here one day. But in all reality, I know that my number will come up, but I don't know where it is in line. It's funny. Just think about it for one moment. Do you hear people saying how they were just speaking with someone yesterday and today they are gone? Well, that's life—gone in a blink of an eye. I used to wish that there was some way that I could speak to those who are no longer here with us, I mean the ones who themselves didn't think that when they had dinner Monday night, that Tuesday would be there last day on this earth. And knowing that I cannot, I just wonder what their last thought was and feelings were on that day. I used to always wonder when my turn will come. How old will I be? Will I get the opportunity to know how old? Or will it happen so quickly that I won't know? It's strange.

That's how I feel about the hundreds of elderly folks I've taken care of. As I told you about earlier in the book, about the man whose hand I held while he made his transition over. What were his last thoughts? What were his last wishes? Although he couldn't talk, I'd be willing to bet that he had plenty he would have liked to say but couldn't. This is one reason why I made it a practice to thank God for each day I'm blessed to be here on earth. He holds the keys to whether I will enter his kingdom or not. He is the only one who can say when my time here is over. You really have got to live each day as if it's your last because you really never know. Make someone smile just for the sake of smiling. Go visit a nursing home, bring someone's mother who gets no visitors flowers, or tell a stranger in the supermarket how nice that color looks on them or how nice the color of their eyes or hair is. Believe me, you'll get more joy from doing this than you can imagine, and at the same time, you've brightened someone else's day too. We are all so busy running and trying to get to a job or get home to be a couch potato with a slice of pizza in our hands, but most of us never even think about how sad someone we know may be feeling or how sick someone may be feeling. You've noticed that they seem different. Take the time to say, "Hello, how are ya today?" Just those simple words alone may make that person's day. Spread a little sugar around sometimes and leave the salt at home. When you crack an egg, make sure you examine the yoke very carefully. You may find sadness, gladness, depression, or a lot of madness.

But make sure you examine it carefully. You never know what's to be found. Let's face it, we all are gonna get old. Some of us will be blessed enough to still remain in the right frame of mind, and but some are not so lucky. Once an adult, twice a child—will you experience being young again, young like a child? Age can only tell. I hope you live well.

It's Good to Be Queen in Oklahoma City

This particular caregiving job took place in Oklahoma City. I was living in Atlanta, Georgia, when I was offered this job. I don't know how they found me. I can't even remember how I got the job. Anyway, they flew me into Oklahoma City for the job. When I arrived in OKC, I met a little lady named Lilly. The diagnosis on Lilly was that she had Alzheimer's, and I was told that through word of mouth, these folks heard about me and liked what others had to say about the care I gave to the elderly. I noticed right away that she resembled someone I had already taken care of in the past. I really went to this interview expecting the worst and wondered why these folks got me all the way out of Atlanta when Oklahoma was full of caregivers and qualified nurses. I can tell you that it sure did pump up my ego, thinking I was the best. How could I say no to these folks? After all, she did look familiar, and I kind of liked the way Oklahoma City was looking. She seemed to be very quiet and laid-back. They paid nearly $1,200 for a plane ride out there. I kinda felt like I owed them after they spent so much money and were willing to pay my fees. So back in Atlanta, I went to pack my things and go right back to start the job. After I returned back to the job, things seemed to go pretty well. I learned quickly that the queen went to the beauty shop weekly to get hair and nails done. I also took her out once or twice per week to her favorite restaurant. As the job went on, I started to notice things about the queen that seemed to be more mental than someone with Alzheimer's. She started to do really scary things, like grabbing the steering wheel while I was driving. We would go to a family buffet on Sundays, and this was the gathering place for people coming from church. It was usually packed, but I'd always get dinner for the two of us so she wouldn't have to stand in a long line. It would be better for her at ninety-four to sit and wait. On this Sunday, the queen decided that after I excused myself to go to the bathroom, she was too hot and started taking her clothing off in the middle of this restaurant with about one hundred people eating there that day. Did I get a surprise upon returning to the dining room! There the queen was standing in the middle with everything off except her underwear. I thought, *What the heck has she done?* And there was a sweet little lady trying to help get her clothing back on. I had to mentally get myself together to try to handle this; so as I walked over, the little lady, whose name I didn't get, quickly asked, "Honey, do you know her? Is she with you?" I quickly responded, "Unfortunately yes, she is," in a stern and grunting voice. "Thank you for your help," I said, as the entire restaurant of people watched in disbelief, and I could even hear a few of them laughing in the distance.

Part Two: It's Good to Be Queen

As I struggled to talk Lilly into getting her clothing back on, she quickly said, "Nope, I'm not gonna do it!" Can you imagine what was going through my mind? I knew already that she was very controlling and demanding, and this is one challenge that I would be losing. It was so sad, and we had such a huge audience; so as I nicely asked the queen to put her clothing back on, the louder she said, "No, I'm not gonna do it!" At this point, I wanted to just put them back on her myself or leave her there, which I knew I could not do. So instead of making an even bigger scene than she already had, we slowly walked out of the restaurant with her naked and with me the color red. We left our meals that hadn't been touched. As we walked out, two of the most handsome men were on their way in. On that day, I looked very attractive, I'd say. But in disbelief and with eyes the size of eight balls, these two watched and wondered, *Was there something more being served at the restaurant that day?* And if there was, the looks on their faces said, "We don't want any." Fortunately for me, I parked very close to the door that day. We didn't have far to walk. She got in, and all was quiet on the drive home. I drove us as she sat back, with a kinda cat that swallowed the canary smile on her face. Don't ask what look I had on mine. As we got to her home, I was so frozen with disbelief I could not do a thing. I left her to get out of the car and walk inside all alone; after all, she was not going to do what I asked her to do anyway. Now I knew why they couldn't get anyone in that entire city to care for this lady. They had depleted their leads for a caregiver. As a matter of fact, the whole town knew the queen. Everywhere we went, folks would ask me if I was staying with her long and that they knew her history with the agencies and hospitals. She had run her course. No one would even think of caring for her. That day at the restaurant after returning home, she finally got out of the car and walked inside naked. I reported the incident to her children, and that was that. After another five or six stripping incidents, I knew that this lady was mentally ill and did not have Alzheimer's. After a while, she decided I was not going to leave, and she stopped trying to run me away. In the end, we became best friends. I always liked her, but I hated her ways of trying to get rid of me. Twenty-nine others before me ran away over the past year, I was told; but I stood my ground, and the queen finally backed down and lost her crown. A year went by, and Lilly became very ill and passed away. I must say that in the end, even with all the tricks she pulled, I missed my friend. And for her it was good to be queen. She told me that if she passed to dress her as if she were going shopping, and that's what I did. She had her purse earrings, hair and nails done as usual, and all her favorite pieces of jewelry. Queeny liked to shop and liked to be pampered. I must say she had very good taste. Who knows, heaven probably had plenty of things for her that fit her taste—plenty of things fit for a queen. Although it was a great challenge for me working with this lady, with a little patience, understanding, love, and concern, we became two good friends. So long, queen, so long.

Chapter 5

Once an Adult, Twice a Child

You know, we are born into this great place we call a universe. We have no choice in picking who our parents will be. We can't be born and say, "Oh, I'd like to live in a rich family. I want to get everything I want, from the best quality of baby clothing, the best schools, and best college out there." We can't make our parents become judges, doctors, or famous TV personalities. We just have to accept who God brought together to bring us into this world or even sometimes who God didn't bring together to bring us into this world. But one thing is true: we get here. I'm sure most of us would just be happy as a lamb to be born into wealth. It may make some of us very selfish and do very selfish, unimportant things with our wealth. Or some of us may choose to use our wealth to help others. Which one would you choose to be? Then we will always have those people whose strongest desire is to get and keep as much money as they can and not help one soul even if their lives depended on it. I've met and still do know a few of these types. All I can do is feel sadness for them. As the Bible states, they know not what they do. And again some of them know and couldn't care less. They want to secure every nickel and dime they can. And somehow they really in their minds think that they are safe. That's always been so funny to me. Now it may keep them safe with the obligations we all have every day to survive in this world; but it is so selfish to believe that money, denado, lira, pesos, benjamins, and grants will really keep them safe. How could it? We are living in very trying and scary times. Life on this planet is getting to be more and more uncertain. We're here today but maybe gone tomorrow. We're born unaware, without responsibility, depending solely on another to feed us and keep us clean and safe. Then we grow to an adult. We've learned to care for ourselves and do things on our own from the parents God gave us. Some of us go through life with lots of wealth and are a great service to mankind while others think of nothing but how they can get more cash. Soon after we've lived an exciting life, we've done it all. Now we are old and lonely; the party is over. All our friends are gone or deceased. We find ourselves losing our memory, forgetting how to do things like tying our own shoes. We find that we need help to live our daily life. If you think about it, it may even seem that we just went through a revolving door. We were born not knowing how to do anything, totally dependent on someone else. We go right back to where we started. We were once an adult, and we go right back to being a child. Funny how life brings you right back where you started. Enjoy life, have fun, see all you can see, and be all that you can be. Be everything except selfish. After all, who do we really think we are fooling?

Who Cares for the Caregiver?

As a caregiver, we have many challenges we sometimes wonder, "Who will take care of me? Will I lose my mind caring for these folks?" This job is so tough. Every day you expect something new. It will leave you wondering what you should do. There's a new challenge in your every move: people trying to leave, you trying to bring them back, or getting someone into bed who doesn't want to go. You're now into three hours, and they want to remain up, so you end up giving in. Sometimes there are those who are dependent on you for using the bathroom, and there are accidents, and you have to change hats and become a housekeeper or cleaning lady. It's now dinnertime, time for hat number two. You sometimes have to feed the person you're caring for. A lot of times they can't remember how to eat on their own. Some of them even lose the ability to chew, so now their meals have to be put in a blender. They're now on a puree diet. This is so they can swallow easier. We as caregivers rarely get the normal eight hours of sleep. I can remember when I cared for six alone. I think I was getting by on about three hours per night. I really didn't know what danger I was putting myself in. You must get your rest. We do laundry, make beds, put clothing away, hand out medications, give baths, etc. There was always someone trying to leave; in my case, at least day and night, I was bringing someone back inside. By the time I got one seated, two more were trying to leave. I personally feel that caregiving is one of the hardest jobs out there, and I also feel that caregivers should be paid more than what a lot of them are receiving. People depend on us to care for their moms, dads, aunts, and uncles. But a lot of them still do not want to pay more for the care of their loved one. Most folks will go more than minimum wage but not very much more. They need to know how hard this work is and be more considerate to what the caregiver is going through when they are assisting the one who needs care. A lot of clients are on medications that should slow down some of the anxiety that their loved one is going through. But also a lot of times, what we think will calm a person down when they're really agitated will end up doing the opposite and cause them to get even more agitated resulting in a hard day for the caregiver. The doctor then needs to order a different med that is right for that client. I've found that most folks with Alzheimer's do not like to take baths. They don't even like water on them unless it's to drink. I really don't know why. It always seems to be a fearful thing for them. But a lot of times even though they may not want to get into the bath or shower, you've still gotta keep them clean, so you have to find a way to get them into the shower. A lot of the time they will fight you because they don't want to get in. Then this becomes a very hard task to handle. A lot of people with Alzheimer's are very combative and will surely show their muscle if they are feeling forced to do something they don't want to do. So the best thing to do is back off and try again later or in a few minutes. When we are dealing with people with Alzheimer's, you must be gentle and warm with these folks. Shouting or loud talking sometimes will frighten or even sometimes scare them away. Unless they have some type of hearing impairment, there is no need to talk loudly to them. Speaking in a normal voice is good enough. You don't want to come off as making them feel as if something is terribly wrong with them. Although you already know that they have this disease, there is no reason to rub it in their face and treat them like children. Who cares for the caregiver? Really, you have to take care of yourself. Have your spouse or significant other give you a back rub. Work out. Get a membership at the gym. That's what kept me going. Pamper yourself every break you get. Eat well. When I say well, I mean right—eat the right things with lots of fruits and vegetables. Drink lots of water. Don't forget to dress well when you can. Make it a point to get out of that caregiver suit and get into a dress or something. Dress up every once in a while so you don't forget that person you always were under the caregiver clothing. Sometimes we let caregiving take us down to where we are starting to look like the client literally because of our attire. We get comfortable with the look and feel of sweats and sneakers and become too tired to dress up or even put a little lipstick on. Don't forget you or who you are. Unfortunately, this is that person's destiny. You're only there to make their lives easier and happier. You're not there to take their place. I know that may seem somewhat harsh, especially for those of you who are really, really close to your loved one; but it's only the cold hard truth.

First Date with Alzheimer's

When I first started taking care of people with middle-stage Alzheimer's, I thought this was so funny but at the same time sad. To tell you the truth, I didn't know what to think of the whole thing. I really thought that this was some sort of mental illness than what everyone called Alzheimer's. People were literally joking about the disease, calling it old-timer's disease, Alzheimer's, old people's disease, and so on. So really at that time, I thought that it was a disease that only the old got around the age of sixty. When I started taking care of them, I'd often find it funny. These folks would have me laughing all the time even when I was chasing someone trying to bring them back inside the house. I had folks asking me if wasn't tired or crazy. How could it be any fun taking care and running these folks down all day? I was just a natural-born caregiver. That's why it didn't bother me so much. Now there were times when I was overwhelmed with tiredness from being up all night with someone who had sundowners. But after I had rested, it was on again. What some folks were crying about because of stress, I was truly enjoying. It was almost a study for me. I'd sit and have conversations with these people, knowing that this conversation was not going to have any real direction or meaning. It was just fun to see how far they could go or remember. Sometimes we'd even laugh about something that totally made no sense whatsoever. And it was funny how they could catch themselves, laughing at themselves, making that mistake too, and in an instance not remembering that they laughed about it. You could really get tangled up there if you didn't watch it. Do you know that there were times that I'd talk to one of these folks, and for about five minutes, I'd get the most normal conversation? Then there were those that I'd talk to, and it would be as if I were talking to myself, and it could really get frustrating. I'd love to let them help with the laundry. Someone would always manage to make a game out of the whole thing. Someone would take a sheet or towel and throw it up in the air and let it fall down over their head just like a three-year-old. I'd watch with a smile on my face, just looking at the children playing. Some have a spot of memory for special thoughts, it seemed, when others had none saved at all. I always used to think that everyone's disease was the same. But nope, not exactly true. Sure, they all have been diagnosed with this horrid disease, but some really displayed many different moods. I took care of a lady with midstage Alzheimer's that could count to twenty and beyond. She could still write her name nicely and carry on a pretty good conversation every once in a while. I questioned her family many times about whether or not they were sure that she had Alzheimer's, and according to them, she had it for quite some time. I was just so amazed at some of the things she could do with the length of time she has had Alzheimer's. After working and being around these folks for almost half of my life, I started to wonder if it was rubbing off on me. Really, after a while, you get very forgetful and start to question yourself. Wait a minute. Am I getting Alzheimer's? A lot of times I couldn't find my keys and would go to the fridge; and there they would be, nice and cold. I found that I was starting to do the same things they were doing, forgetting at times what I had for dinner. Then at the end of the day, when all were in bed, I remembered I had no dinner. Honey, this is not Alzheimer's. It was burnout. You better take a little time off. I really stress time off for you a lot because it's so important. Your mind will play some crazy little tricks on you after a while. That's when you'll know you've had a long date with Alzheimer's. Go and date something else for a while and come back later.

Grocery Shopping We Will Go

Oh no, she didn't. I decided to take Grace to the grocery store with me. She was a favorite and a sweet little lady, but honey, Grace did me wrong today! I was bent down to get the mayo from the lower shelf, and when I stood back up, Grace had disappeared. Now this was something I was quite used to but not today, Grace. It's raining outside. Please, please be in the store somewhere and not outside, lost in the rain. I quickly left my shopping cart and ran to the customer service booth to let them call for Grace over the loudspeaker. She was not there. As tears welled up in my eyes with fear in my heart, I had it now. Grace's family were gonna get on me. What harm would come to poor Grace outside in that rainy weather? The thoughts kept coming. What if we don't find her? What if she gets in the car with a psycho? Now by looking at Grace, you'd think that she was just as normal as you and me. That's until you tried a normal conversation with her. As the store attendant and I sat out looking for Grace, all I could hear is "Get away" loudly. "You damn nut, get outta my shopping cart." Apparently, Grace had started to eat the grapes out of a not-so-nice or understanding lady's cart. My god, the store had plenty more where those came from. Oh well, you know how some people are about their fruit. Grace had mouthed a good amount of this lady's grapes and proceeded to walk away with the lady's purse. Well, I was so thankful to have found her and wasn't really thinking about the other person, but I finally realized that this lady was difficult, and I would apologize for Grace and let her know of Grace's condition. I was sure she'd understand, and we'd be on our way. Well, no, this lady had to show us what she was made of; and mind you, her English was awful. She continually said, "You get her outta here. She no good. She take all my grapes. She crazy lady. I tell police on her and you too. Oh, crazy lady, she thief. She steal wallet." No matter what or how I apologized, the home girl wasn't having it. She was angrier about the grapes than her wallet. Poor Grace, in her mind she was taken back in time a little. She was in the store doing her own shopping, and the cart was hers, and so was the purse. I don't know how, but somehow in her mind she was still living in her home. I don't know! She may have thought she was grocery shopping for her family. Long-term memory kind of kicked in from her past. The store manager took over the situation nicely and sent us on our way. By the way, we didn't get groceries on that day. On our way out, all I could hear was "No, she no good. She steal my grapes." I was somewhat embarrassed, but in my mind, I was laughing so very hard. Poor Grace had forgotten all this so quickly. Some people are so rude no matter how much I explained about Grace's condition. All this lady could still do was to think of her grapes. Now that just took the whole bottle of grape juice. A lot of people don't know about this disease and still consider a person like Grace to be mentally ill or just plain crazy. No matter what you say to them, they have their minds made up about that person. Alzheimer's can be so heartbreaking for the caregiver, whether you're a hired long-term caregiver or a relative. People just don't understand or just don't want to try to or just plain don't care as long as it's not affecting their lives. Hey, wake up, people. Someone with Alzheimer's is a person too. So don't be cruel. This could be, as I reiterate, you!

And the Teeth Came at Me

Mrs. Dorothy—how could she be wrong? Nothing this lady said was wrong. You see, she was one of those people who knew it all. Her way or the highway, Alzheimer's or not. She loved to yell at me. My cooking was always rotten, didn't taste good. But only she'd be talking with her mouth full of my horrible cooking and not missing a bite. And she always cleaned her plate. Mrs. Dorothy loved to play the race game. She'd get in my face and ask me how I was, and then here it came. I knew it was coming sooner or later. This time, she asked why my skin was so dark, how it got that way. She'd say, "What happened to you?" And I'd say, "Oh no, Dorothy, when they were dipping everyone in that creamy, good-tasting chocolate, did they forget you? Oh no! You missed it. What are you gonna do now?" And she'd actually really stop and think for a second, wondering if this really happened or not. Then I'd say, "You better run down to the factory and tell them they forgot to dip you." She'd think about it and say, "Oh, you bitch, that's not true." And I'd just laugh. That really pissed her off. This lady was a real pest that just wouldn't go away. She'd get in my face and look at me eyeball to eyeball; and she'd just be cussing at me, only I didn't understand one word she said most times because her teeth were going in and out, as if they were going to fall out. She was so angry that her dentures were moving back and forth. At that point, I'd have to gain control while bursting with laughter deep inside or she'd go on and on. Enough was enough; and I'd send her to her room until she could act like a lady, I'd say, instead of a little child. Dorothy was a very mean lady and a manipulator. Sometimes I wondered if she even had Alzheimer's. She'd come in, and she would be so nice to me. But you can bet that by the end of the day, she was going to make a remark about my color. She seemed to really get a kick out of it. She would never use adhesive to keep her teeth secure. This is why when she talked, they moved in and out. Sometimes they'd really just fall in her lap. She'd just pick them up and put them right back in. I don't know why color was such an issue for her. She had full authority to say no as far as the hire of caregiver went. Sometimes I thought that maybe someone African American did something wrong to her, and now she hated all African American people. I thought about asking her this several times, but in the end, I just decided not to waste my energy trying to change her. She has Alzheimer's anyway. It would be wiser to just be her friend and do my job, and maybe one day she'd see that I'm not that person who did her wrong. If she just hated blacks, I'd show her that everyone is not the same and that I was truly a great, caring caregiver. Even though she made my job very hard, I still found the time to give great care and do the job I was there for. I talked to Dorothy's children several times about the name calling, but that stubborn Dorothy would even call them names if they tried stopping her. And believe me, she called them worse things than she called me. But it was

.ce. They did warn me about her when I
.e job, and they did tell me about her and
.:e game and didn't seem to know why she
started that. I just told them she hadn't just started it. It was always there. She just decided to start it up again with me. She was just plain hateful. I found out long ago you don't throw salt at salt. It's better to throw sugar no matter how ugly. If you keep it up long enough, you just may find you've finally made something very sweet. I've done a lot of caregiving in my life, and some of these folks were sweeties, and some were downright devils. But one thing I never let any one of my clients do was run me away. Some put pressure on so hard that I nearly hung up my coat, but that's what they'd want in the first place, so I wouldn't. Soon enough I'd find that they really liked me, and when it was time to go, they didn't want me to leave. I took a lot off Dorothy. I watched those teeth flop around for many months. But in the end, she finally stopped the name calling. She didn't use the color word so much, and she managed to see if she could be my friend. In the end, she lost those old teeth, and we decided to let her go toothless for a while; it seemed they were anxious to leave her mouth anyway, and it didn't stop her from eating. Those gums were as tough as her mouth, and she didn't miss those teeth either.

From Where Did the Name Alzheimer's Come From?

You know, I've taken care of so many folks with Alzheimer's disease and never really thought anything of the name itself. Then one day as the residents and I sat around watching old movies on this cold winter day, I sat back and just kind of looked at them and wondered, *Where did that name Alzheimer's come from? Who was he/she, or was it just a name a doctor gave to patients when he/she didn't know what else to name the disease he/she had diagnosed?* So I decided to do a little research to try to find out and put my curiosity to rest. After searching, I finally found that Alzheimer's wasn't just a made-up name some doctor labeled his patients with. Dr. Alois Alzheimer was the first doctor to discover this horrid disease in a woman by the name of Auguste D. after reading her medical information. He became so taken away that he had to follow up with it and research her condition, and this is where the name Alzheimer's came from. Mrs. Auguste D. became the first patient to be studied and labeled with his name, a name now globally used and respected. In 1886, the twenty-two-year-old young man who was born in the southern part of Germany graduated from medical school. He had a passion to study histology (the study of human tissues), epilepsy, brain tumors, Huntington's disease, syphilis, and dementia at that time. There are so many different kinds of diseases out there I was always interested in, like actual death, although death itself is not a disease. I always had an interest to know why a person was so cold when they were dead, but I was only a child at the tender age of sixteen. When I bent down to kiss my dear mother at her funeral and she was so cold, I needed to know why. What had they done to her? When I became a woman, I made it my goal to become a mortician so I could find out what went on. But sadly I never started the classes. And ultimately, Alzheimer's became more fascinating to me. This is why I took a strong interest in this disease and the care of people with it, not just the enjoyment I got from caring for these folks. I really also needed to know what and why and how this disease came to be. There are still a lot of unanswered questions, but that too will take time as everything does. Dr. Alzheimer was such a young man with interest in such a difficult disease, but because of his strong interest in Auguste D. and needing to know how the disease affected her and where it came from, he pursued his interest and studied until he started to get answers. At the age of twenty-four, he got a job as an asylum officer at a mental institution. This is where he first met Auguste D. as she became the first patient in the world with this disease now called Alzheimer's.

Warning Signs of Alzheimer's

Now we all probably have gone to Walmart, came out, and couldn't find our car. We even forget where we put our keys. That's a biggie for me, and I can usually find them still in the door lock or still in the car door or trunk after getting the groceries out. And gosh have I been lucky. They usually remain there until the next day when I need to go out. With Alzheimer's, it's a little different. Do you ever find yourself repeating the same things over and over, and finally realizing you've said this already? Or driving in your car and forgetting what road to take home? Do you have to pull over to figure it out or end up taking three hours to get there when it should have taken you fifteen minutes? What about hiding things from your own self or forgetting how to do a simple thing like turn the stove off or on? All of a sudden, it pops back into your memory. What about something as regular as counting your money, something we do each day, putting your shirt on right instead of inside out? Or having beliefs of something so farfetched you just know it can't be real like you've won a lot of money? Have you forgotten that you've already put your socks on? Can't remember if you ate dinner? These are just a few examples. There are plenty of others that I haven't mentioned, but I'd say if you're experiencing any of these symptoms or many of these, see your health care provider right away. Sit down and discuss your feelings and concerns with him or her and let them get test done for you to rule it out or in. It seems to me to be a sneaky disease. It sneaks up and robs you of your mind, the most precious part of our human being. As I said before, it's a bright light that slowly fades to black. As scary as it is, a lot of the time the ones who are stricken with this disease are in denial for quite some time. I've even dealt with a person who had Alzheimer's for quite some time and was still in strong denial; and if you'd bother to tell her, she'd laugh as if you were just so crazy to say that about her. She'd say, "Oh, I'm so ashamed of you.

Shame on you! I thought you had more respect for me than that." And she would be really truly hurt. But what I couldn't get was she would be the one to ask me what was wrong with her, or my family told me I'm sick, am I? And with what? She'd say. There are medications out there to slow down this disease but unfortunately none yet to stop it. But I guess if it were me who had it, I think I'd want to try whatever meds they had out to try just to hold on to my memory for as long as possible and remember those I loved for as long as I could. The saddest part of this disease for me is when you start to forget your loved ones; it must be so scary to not recognize your own children when you're slowly forgetting their faces. You know you know them, but you just can't put your finger on if you know them very personally as family or if they are a friend you've forgotten. This would really frighten me. I don't ever want to forget my sweet little girl's face or my son's smiling face. Oh, just the thought of this scares me, and it's not even happening to me yet. It breaks my heart when I see family members cry because their wife, mother, or dad doesn't know them anymore, ask them who they are, or call them as someone else. When you feel in your mind that it's automatic, they know their own children. But then reality it has to set in, and you have to really grasp the truth that they no longer remember your face. It's very sad but true, and it's something that the family will eventually have to accept. Not only is the patient in strong denial after diagnosis, sometimes the family is too, depending on how close of a family they may be. So if you notice that your family member is becoming forgetful a lot and do things they don't normally do, I think it's time to get a really good check out, I say, not up. I say out because a checkup is just a physical examination; a check out in my opinion is checking out things other than the norm, things that are a lot more serious.

Getting Enough Exercise

I'm not by any means a doctor or personal trainer. But I know a little about staying physically active. I love to work out, lift weights, and run—anything that will keep my body lean and strong. I get such a wonderful feeling after running and sweating. I literally feel like a new person, a weight lifted off my shoulders. I personally feel that doing physical activity and eating the proper foods can be your friend in warding off Alzheimer's or dementia. Taking a brisk walk for fifteen to thirty minutes three times per week can help with some body aches and really start to build up your self-esteem too. So try to only get involved in the activities you enjoy the most, not the ones you see everyone else is doing. Pick the ones you like, and you'll have better results because you'll be doing the ones you enjoy doing, and then it won't feel like work or being forced to exercise when you really don't feel like it. You'll look forward to it. Exercise can also help with several diseases. Diabetes is a big one, along with depression and cardiovascular disease. So put on those sneakers and run for a while. If running will be hard for you in the beginning, start out walking at a fast pace. And soon you'll see that you are running with no problem. From my experience of taking care of dying people, people who just insisted on sitting around doing nothing all day seemed to pass on pretty fast. In the meantime, the ones who were very active while with Alzheimer's seemed to outlive these couch-potato types. Even if you are sitting in a wheelchair, some kind of movement is great! Leg exercise, arms—you can still get fit. Use your head to save your mind. Always use protective head gear and eye gear if you're bike riding or playing racket ball, or something of that sort. Getting hit in the head and risking some sort of brain injury, especially if you are older, around the age of sixty-five to seventy, would be really awful for an already-aging brain. That is just what my research found, and I think just common sense could figure this out. Getting hit in the head could be very detrimental, so a cheap investment in a bike helmet would be a wise choice in slimming your chances of getting dementia. You know, I've never asked any of these relatives in the past, but I often wonder now if some of these moms and dads did play sports or got hit in the head at some time in their life. I'm wondering if the blow to their head may have played a big part in the dementia or Alzheimer's they now have. Wouldn't that be something if studies could find this out? No matter how it may have occurred, this disease is very complicated and I think misunderstood, especially by society. People who aren't aware of the disease or care to know about it really should get educated about it. Most of the time, they end up calling these folks when they meet them in person ugly names like they are crazy or nutty and so on simply because they haven't taken the time to see what's really going on. Why? Again, it's not affecting them. It's a sad world we live in.

Stay Stress-free

Anyone who knows me well will tell you what a chronic worrier I was. I'd worry about other folks' problems that didn't even concern me whatsoever. And I think that came from being a chronic people pleaser. Over the years, I've trained myself to stop worrying, especially about the things I had no control over. Looking back, I said to myself, "Okay, girl, you had to be crazy." I always wanted to fix everyone else's problems and wanted everyone to be happy. And this started from around age ten years old till about age forty. And had I not got very angry about a situation, I'd probably still be here worrying about the world. I didn't know that I was playing a possibly detrimental game. Stress can kill. I'd worry so badly that I was up all night sometimes in the fetal position, trying to figure out what was impossible and I had no control over. I used to always have a tummy ache, always breaking out with acne. Finally, I worried so much that I was throwing up green all the time. I couldn't eat. I was afraid to. If I did, I'd suffer great pain. My gosh, don't let it be a glass of milk or ice cream, which

I loved so much! I finally started checking into doctors trying to find out what was ailing my belly. Finally after getting an upper and lower GI series, I found that I had 250 gallstones. I think I broke a record, and this was my grand prize for worrying. It made me somewhat mad when I knew I got this way mostly by worrying about my siblings. I always felt like I had to take care of them while they probably didn't spill one thought about me or my problems. I'm sure most of you aren't like me, but this is what stress can get you. Besides strokes and, over years, chronic stress, these things can do damage to your organs. Try to stay away from folks who get your blood boiling and stay around people who have a calming effect on you like folks at church. These are people who are slow to anger. With blood pressure going up, bitterness, gossiping all the time about things that are upsetting, you're just merely setting yourselves up for a heart attack, a lot of things, even death. So be careful because getting dementia, and possibly Alzheimer's, is right in the center here someplace. Again, this is just from observing people over the years. Crossword puzzles and card games are all good activities to keep our minds flowing and healthy. Try gardening and reading. Try to stay positive. Now this was one of the toughest for me, goodness. The people I associated with had a lot to do with me not being positive about life. When I was worrying about pleasing them, I found out that they were very jealous of me and harboring negative and hateful thoughts about me too, All the while, that negative energy was all around me, and I was too naive to notice it. Be careful.

Setting a Plan for Prevention: Diet

If you are headed toward the elderly years and you may have not always had a good diet or ate things essential to your good health, now may be a good time to start. A lot of us go through early adulthood eating everything simply because we feel that since we are young and vibrant, we don't have to worry about eating right. It's good to start right from the beginning. Just because you're young does not put an untouchable stamp on your life. If you have an elderly person in your home who is fortunate enough to not have any ailments or serious diseases, pat them on the back. That's great. Why not encourage them to eat better starting now? I'm no nutritionist or dietician. But I've worked with all different types of folks over the years. I've learned to eat better myself because of the strict diets some of them had to have, and since I was a diabetic, I too had to be careful. Since I was careful, I went to the doctor one day and got a clean bill of health saying that I was no longer a diabetic. So I must have been doing something right! Encouraging your loved one to eat right starting now could possibly stop this dreaded disease Alzheimer's or dementia from even bothering their livelihood.

Eat fewer saturated fats.

Eat more fish and healthy fats (omega-3).

Eat more fruits and vegetables. Blueberries are very good.

Take vitamins and minerals, like antioxidants. Consult with your doctor to see which ones are best for your health.

Lower sodium intake or try a different salt, perhaps sea salt. I always use lemon juice as a replacement for salt.

Restrict your daily calories.

If you must enjoy alcohol, enjoy it in moderation.

Exercise and engage in stress-relieving activities. As I mentioned before, don't just sit around being a couch potato. Get busy living or get busy dying— such a true and wonderful statement.

Go out and join a seniors club. There are plenty of them around and most of the time will provide the transportation for you if you have transportation problems. Don't be afraid to ask your doctor about where to find these types of places.

Choose activities that stimulate your mind. Take part in group reading or read alone to keep your mind moving. Find a group that participates in gardening. Planting flowers, with all the beautiful colors and smells, will be very stimulating to the mind and senses.

Volunteer work is a great way to keep that body going and a good way to get out and be around others. You can make new friends and even learn something new.

Getting out of the house will block any chances of getting depressed and bored and will help you to maintain a positive outlook on life.

Try to find a volunteer job close in your neighborhood if long trips are not for you. Also by staying near home, you can have a chance to give back to your community. In any case, try to stay as active as you can. Always eat good foods that contribute goodness to your health. Eat the right foods and stick to them. Reading labels on the packages is always good, and this will ensure that you make wise choices about what you are putting in your body. Now we all sneak a burger here and there, a piece of chocolate cake, but try to save these things for special times or just a special treat. Your body will thank you for it later.

Darla in Georgia

There once was a little lady named Darla. Darla was right at the ripe old age of one hundred years. As

I interviewed Darla about what it was that helped her to nearly get to that ripe old age, the first thing she said was "Well, my mother always told me to eat the right foods and chew my food at least fifteen to twenty times. Now I don't think that I have ever chewed my food but maybe five times if that, so embarrassed to say. Really, I'm a very fast eater, always seemed to just want to get it over." I took Darla's advice and went home and prepared my dinner and tried to chew it at least the fifteen times. I must say by the time I hit ten, I was near gagging. Yuck! I couldn't do it. Just couldn't. It made me feel as if I had regurgitated my food, and we all know how gross that is. But this little lady also told me that she rarely had an upset stomach or stomachache and had really never experienced much constipation. And my question to her was did she think because she chewed her food up so finely, and that making it pass through so smoothly, caused her to never have any ailments? She said yes, and I thought about that, and it did make a lot of sense to me. Now I've always heard that you're supposed to chew a number of times, but I didn't remember how many. After researching it, I did find that twenty is the correct amount, which I would never imagine doing. Now this lady actually did chew that many times, and I remember sitting and waiting and watching her still chewing a mouthful when I'd long chewed mine five minutes ago. I remember getting very restless and a little agitated at having to sit and watch her and also having to reheat her plate a number of times until she was finished. If she hadn't been so sweet, I probably would have tried some way to speed things up. But I thought, *Boy, if that's what's keeping this lady alive and healthy all this time, then more power to her.* She may have taken longer than most, but maybe if I had known and could eat her way, I might not have the stomach ailments I have today. So I thought it was better to take that wisdom and move on and tell others her story. Maybe this will help someone. I've met so many elderly folks that are in ripe old ages, mostly one year short of one hundred years old and some short of one hundred and two. Their stories weren't all about eating all the best foods to live such a long life, although I will always promote that. But the stories I got from them as far as what gave them long life was along the lines of I had a shot of whiskey before bed each night or I drank two glasses of red wine at dinner each night. I even had a hundred-year-old male tell me that all it took for him was a good game of golf regularly. I said, "Well, I know God is at the driver's seat." But I ended my curiosity about this to be God driving and them listening to his daily orders and closely following his recipe. Oh, and let me not forget a biggie that took me years to master. Be a calm person. Don't worry about things you can't fix. Let it go. If it ain't broke, then don't try to fix it. Steer clear of gossip and fake people. After all, who wants to be around people who really don't have your best interest at heart? I think it would be great if all of us had a robot that walked alongside us every day, snatching back all the bad things that we attempt to eat, but we know that this is far from reality. So we as elderly folk, and those of us who are closely becoming elderly, should just try to remember how valuable our frail life is and how blessed some of us are to have reached such a long life. And those of us who haven't quite got there, just treat your bodies right and know that you will get there too. As we grow older, our bodies' needs and wants change anyway. It seems we don't need as much food as we did as when we were young when we'd eat a whole whopper; and now that we are older, we probably prefer one-half of that whopper than a whole one. So eat right. Don't try to fight it. Realize that we are here on this earth for a short time even if we do live to be one hundred. Enjoy it while you're here. Why not? Look good and feel good for as long as your body is good. And that can be a long, long time, if you just do the right thing. Take care of yourself.

A Poem for You?

I no longer know where I'm going, can't remember where I've been. Through all this I'm asking that you'll still be my friend.

When I come down the hall with one shoe on, please don't yell at me, or stare at me long.

Don't pity me, when I try to say your name, and can't remember it, nor can register it in my brain.

This dreaded disease that has conquered my soul, strangled my mind, and put it on overload, wasn't my choice, nor was it a game. It was just something that happened, and I will never be the same. When I call you Betty and your name is Bob, please don't be upset or walk out and nod.

I wish that I could bring back those happy days, when we used to laugh, and used to sing, we used to sniff the flowers that we each would bring.

When you come to see me, please don't cry because all I can do is wonder why. Don't waste your tears when I won't have a clue. Don't make me feel something's wrong with you.

Don't try to tell me, again and again, when I won't understand,

What I won't extend, just hold my hand, and be my friend, even if I've forgotten you, this is where we now begin.

I don't know where I've been and don't know where I'll go, but please come and visit me when I'll need you the most.

Please don't talk about me as if I'm no longer here; don't whisper or ignore me when I'm very near. Although I have changed and forgotten your name, think of yesteryear and how far we came.

I'm so glad that I forgot how to say good-bye; now I don't have to wonder why. Why I am without you, why I don't know my name, why?

Although it'll sometimes be harder on you, just remember, there is nothing that I could do.

Oh, I wish I could hold you and say, "It'll be all right. Tomorrow's another day. We must not give up this fight." Irreversible—that's what's been said. The only word I can remember floating around in my head. So long, my friend, my husband, or wife. You see, I'm unable to tell which one you'll be this night.

So just hold me, hug me, and be anyone. I will still accept your warmth and try to feel your love; and on that final day, when it's all said and done, just remember, we had lots of fun.

CHAPTER 6

Through the Caregiver's Eyes

Over the years as a caregiver, I've heard so many caregivers complain about how hard this type of work is and how we caregivers need to get an organization just for us just for our mental status. I'd hear on the news about how a caregiver did a great job for the now-deceased patient she cared for, and that would be about as far as it would get, leaving some of the caregivers bitter that they only got a pat on the back when they felt that they really should have gotten some sort of standing ovation or at least a fat check. There are some employers who really know that this is hard back-breaking work and really feel for their caregivers, so they pay well and give them little extras, but those kinds of employers are few and far between. In my entire career, I've been spoiled at least three times. I am speaking out for all the good caregivers out there who are doing a great job and feel like you are not getting not so much the money you deserve, but the respect you should be getting for the changing of all the wet soiled and poopy depends. The late nights up, the cooking, the cleaning, the bathing, the laundry, the housekeeping, the medication monitoring, and don't let me forget all the putdowns you may sometimes encounter with someone who really has the advanced stages of Alzheimer's—if this is you, all I can say is speak up. Get that glue off your tongue and start talking. Girls, let's talk about some of these jobs if this was one of your experiences. Remember the lady with Alzheimer's who refused to get into the bathtub, and while you were trying to pull those pants down, she was pulling them back up so in the end you had to step on the middle inside of them to hold them firmly down while she was wildly trying to get them back up and the sweat was nearly blinding you from all of the twisting and turning. LOL.

How about the times you were cooking dinner, and people were trying to leave the house, and you had to stop cooking and go and bring them back? And you had no help; you were the only one working that shift or day most likely. What about the long nights that you had to stay up because someone had (sundowners) days and nights mixed up? You have worked the whole day because someone called in sick, so this eight-hour shift has turned to a sixteen-hour shift, and you're walking and sleeping at the same time. Wooh, talking about exhaustion. Now you still have to attend to these folks. The owner says she can't find anyone else to work and she'll pay overtime and you can go to sleep. But how can you when Bob doesn't want to stay asleep but is going to work at a job he had forty years ago and Mae is going home to cook dinner for her husband who's been deceased for thirty years, so she's trying to leave too? And it's now 3:00 a.m., and you probably were able to only squeeze in a nap somewhere for one-half hour. So you're really a walking sack of jittery nerves now. Finally help arrives, and you can now go home. Oh, but wait. Now you've gotta pick up your own children, go home, and almost do the exact thing you did at work. There's no time off for that long night and day. You've gotta be back to work in about eight hours. When do you rest? Your heart starts to pound at work because you're so afraid of that call that the next shift won't be in again. This has happened to me so many times, but fortunately for me, I had no little ones at home. When you've got heavy care patients, boy does it get hectic. A lot of caregivers want a job, but they call in sick a lot because they become so burned out from the struggle they get from those who are difficult to give care to. Don't let me leave out the combative one. A lot of times you may get into squabbles and get hit or even spit on, and it is so hard to stay calm. But you've got to remain professional when you really want to scream. But don't take it personally. Caregivers have a very challenging job. Hats off to all those true caregivers who know what I'm talking about. I'm sure there are more graphic stories than the few I've mentioned here. But if you've been there with me, then you already know what other types of stories there are. I couldn't write this book without saluting you for all the hard work done—heck, we've all done that. Hang in there, girls! Your hard work is noticed, and the word shall get out more about you and the hard work that you do.

Questions about Alzheimer's

Some family of people with Alzheimer's sometimes had a hard time accepting the fact that their loved one will not recover from this disease. For some reason, they think that recovery is close behind. But sorry I will have to inform you once more, even if I am only a caregiver and not a doctor, I have—and I'm sure that many other caregivers have too—the same information about this disease because of the hours we put in over the years caring for a person. Now we may not be able to run any test to assure anyone about one's condition. But as far as answering questions on their well-being and everyday living skills, I feel that we are somewhat the experts in this area. We see things that the doctor probably will never see simply because we are with that person day in and day out. I would like to advise family members to go to the Internet for more info if they feel they need more help in understanding this disease. You can Google ALS.org and find many answers to some questions that still have you puzzled, or you can also call 1-800-272-3900. They have info available about warning signs of this disease, and it is available in about five different languages. So everyone can get their questions answered. Alzheimer's does not discriminate. It will invade anyone's body. Your skin color or religion will have no effect on not getting it. It's everyone's disease, and we all need to fight together to find a cure for it.

Here Are about Seven Stages of Alzheimer's

1. No impairment

2. Very mild decline

3. Mild decline

4. Moderate decline

5. Moderate to severe decline

6. Severe decline

7. Very severe decline

You will notice these declines in your family member if you are closely monitoring them. It seems to sneak up on some, and others don't seem to really feel anything. Then one day it attacks others quickly.

I've seen people who on one day seem just as normal as you and me; then a day or two later, they have made a drastic change in speech, judgment, etc.

Here Are Ten Warning Signs of Alzheimer's

1. Memory loss
2. Poor planning and problem solving
3. Difficulty in completing a task
4. Confusion in time or place
5. Trouble understanding
6. Problems speaking and writing
7. Misplacing things, can't retrace steps
8. Poor judgment
9. Social activities withdrawal
10. Changes in mood

Myths on Alzheimer's

1. Memory loss is a natural part of living.
2. Alzheimer's is not fatal.
3. Only old people get this disease; it can strike people in their thirties, forties, and fifties.
4. Aluminum can cause Alzheimer's.

5. Aspartame causes memory loss, reported in 2006.

6. Flu shots increase risk of getting Alzheimer's.

7. Silver dental fillings increase chances of getting Alzheimer's: 50 percent mercury, 35 percent silver, 15 percent tin.

8. There are treatments to stop Alzheimer's. There's none at present, only medications to slow the process, approximately six to twelve months.

People seem to think that as soon as they can't remember where they parked their car, they may be getting Alzheimer's.

I can remember when AIDS first hit the news, and it spread like wildfire. Everyone had a paragraph to add to the first story they heard. So AIDS had become an immediate death sentence for anyone who touched someone with AIDS, used the same toilet, or hugged someone with AIDS. Well, they're not quite as paranoid about it like AIDS. But I've met quite a few that seem to think just because they can't find their car or forgot where their car keys were. "Oh, I think I'm getting Alzheimer's," they'd say. LOL. It was so funny for me because I knew that almost all of us at a certain age start to forget things a lot. I think it was around forty years of age for me and a few friends of mine. Alzheimer's has that kind of power to frighten anyone. Just the thought of not remembering anything or anyone is horrifying. Just like being blind would frighten me because I always want to see in the mirror what I look like before leaving my home. And that thought of not being able to see my food or what's in it would really scare me. But these two things can't be transferred just that easily! One person can get a rumor going, and a whole town of misinformed people becomes paranoid. Always get the facts before you judge. I think, though, people joke a lot and think Alzheimer's is funny. But when it strikes someone they know on a personal level, it's not so funny at all. Alzheimer's is a really misunderstood disease, and people would rather judge before they research this disease. It is very sad and very heartbreaking. These caregivers who are caring for the folks in the long term become attached to the one they give care to, and soon they become just like their family member. For me it's very personal, especially if that person doesn't have any relatives. That by itself is so heartbreaking for me. As I've taken care of plenty who had no one, I always made it a point to be there for them.

Caregiver versus Nurse

One challenge I had left me upset after each encounter was the visiting nurse. There are plenty of excellent nurses out there. But my experience with one in particular left me with sourness in my mouth. I didn't have the degree or the hours of training that some nurses had, but I had hands-on training that I don't think any nurse could match when it came to caring for our folks with Alzheimer's. It's not a brag, just facts. And please I am by no means trying to make any nurse out there upset or feel belittled. So if you are a nurse and reading my book, don't be upset. This is just my experience with one nurse who drove me bananas.

I didn't get a degree in nursing, but I did know the residents that I cared for. This nurse was to come on a weekly visit to do vitals and just regular checkups on the residents. Well, each time she came, it was vital to get into their personal life: can you remember the last time a resident had sex with their mate who was no longer there and had been deceased for years? This was just hanging around time after she was long supposed to have left. She was so childish she would laugh and joke with the residents as if they truly were kids. Truly some of them had converted back to childhood and laughed with her, but then there were those who didn't care to tell her about such things. Anyway, these folks had Alzheimer's and could barely remember things such as that. As much as I kindly told her to not go into those types of conversations, she'd bring it up every time until I finally had to call her agency who didn't seem to think there was anything wrong with this. But her job was to check on the residents, not check them out by prying into their history. She'd tell me, "Well, in my country, we always spoke of these things." And I kindly would remind her that this was not her country, and that kind of talk must be stopped while she was visiting the residents. She would look into my refrigerator and tell me what was healthiest for them to eat. I sometimes wanted to push her out of the door. Most of her time there was taking blood pressure, which I did regularly to everyone anyway, and the rest of the time she would snack and joke. I could never figure how she was hired as a nurse. She always would cling to one male in the home, who she always had laughing all the time. She would tell him that he didn't have Alzheimer's, and doctors misdiagnosed him. Finally, I got state backup help on replacing this lady. So it turned out that she did leave us, and I later found out that she was well-known in the community because of her horrible bedside manners and that 50 percent of the time she was high on prescription medications. I was always suspicious about her unprofessional style and kidlike manners and wondered why someone hadn't reported her before. I could always catch her nodding when she should have been on her way to her next client. She also tried to get me to not apply deodorant after giving the residents a bath and that in her country she'd say, "We don't use it. It causes cancer." So when I asked what they used for personal hygiene, she said nothing or these crystal rocks that were to be rubbed on the skin. I then told myself, "Oh yeah, she's nuts, all right." And I kindly let her know that in their home they would be using deodorant only. She also insisted that Alzheimer's was a made-up disease by America to scam the insurance companies. She finally got the boot one day when she crossed the line by telling me how my caregiving job was just slavery and that I needed a degree to really be respected and appreciated. I needed to be a nurse. That was the last of her, at least in our home. The reason for this story was even though some great nurses come to the United States, some bring their practices here and want us to follow what they do in their hospitals and homes in their country. But I told her it could not and would not be done. Again, be careful about who tries to care for your mom or dad or relative. Not all who say "Hi, I am a nurse" is a nurse just because they have a degree that says so. It's all in the skills.

End-of-life Care

There was one a lady I cared for whom I'll call Sue. She was a very sweet lady whom I had grown pretty close to in spite of her having Alzheimer's. She still had a quietness about her, kind of laid-back and accepting of everything that was happening to her mind, spirit, and body. She did like to talk. Some days were better and more understood than others. And I felt she had met her match with me because I do have the gift of gab. We were just talking about life one rainy day. I like the rain, and so did she. So we kind of just slid on into things that took place in our lives. I'll never forget her. The wisdom I gained from her really opened my mind to really make me think about what's really, really important in life, something I really hadn't given much thought.

I kinda just went with the flow. As I looked at this eighty-year-old lady, I began to ask her questions. And the most important one I could think of for her was what did she envision her end-of-life care to be? She really had to think for a minute or two. But I was amazed at how she opened up and told me what she expected. She went on to say that she hoped that I would be the one caring for her when that time came. That really made me feel good, and I told her, "Yeah, that would be nice"; but I couldn't make that kind of promise, especially if she got really ill. It would have to be a certified nurse, but who knows, it could be me. She told me how she would like to be kept very warm if it happened in the wintertime and nice and cool in the summer if it was very hot outside. She told me that she'd like someone to read to her once a day books on gardening and the book of Psalm—I thought that that was an interesting mix. She wished to be buried in a pink gown with white roses. And I said to myself that I would surely make sure her family gets this news from me. She expressed how she wanted that day to be a joyful day and not a lot of tears; but this would be hard, I thought, when you really love someone. She said she wanted a happy song played instead of that sad ole funeral music. It only makes the event, she called it, sadder; and I agree. Why should it be so sad? She said that when her mind is completely gone and her memory is no more, she hopes that her body care will be great and that she won't be left in soiled pants. I said to myself right then, "Wow, I hope that there would be a way for me to be there for this lady because all her wishes would come so easy for me while some wouldn't even acknowledge her feelings and just get on with it and put any clothing on her." I asked her if she wanted to keep the lipstick on, and she responded, "I'm wearing it now, aren't I?" And I said, "I guess my question was kinda stupid, huh?" She really placed a lot of emphasis on being treated nicely and cared for, not being abused and left alone. I tried to comfort her by telling her that as nice of a lady that she was, I didn't think she would have to worry about that. After all, she was in her own home, with people around that really loved and cared for her. I told her that I'm sure that the end-of-life care for her would probably be a celebration or party just as she envisioned it. It will be a very great time. How about you all? As you read my book, do you ever think about what your end-of-life wishes would be? I guess probably not. You see, when we are healthy and going about our daily schedules, work, kids, etc., we'd probably find thinking about that type of thing not on the top of our list, especially if we are young in age. And it would be awfully sad to go around worrying about that. Well, don't. Just think about it one day when you've got some downtime, no matter what your adult age is. Just take a moment. After all, no day is promised us. This lady was eighty years of age. She could have just outlived a twenty-year-old. I believe that we all think or feel it's just some type of tradition to live to seventy-five or so. But if you really think about it, we all are on God's time, so we really don't know when we will leave here; and age is no exception. Some of us think we are gonna live forever. When we are really young, we really think like that. Why would we think about passing on? That wouldn't be fair, would it? I mean you're just twenty years old. How could it be your time? God wouldn't be that unfair. I don't think fairness has anything to do with it. Life is funny! You never know when a corner will turn.

Doctors' Appointments

A lot of our elderly, especially those with early stages of Alzheimer's, do not and simply refuse to go to visit the doctor. They can still function quite well, even though they have this disease, and you can't just talk in front of them as if they aren't there. I think it's the fear of hearing that word Alzheimer's over and over. It's like going to get a cut on your back each visit and opening up an old wound over and over again, and they just don't want to hear the doctor tell them of a diagnosis they don't believe is real. Many folks with this disease really just don't care to visit and talk about Alzheimer's at all. I often think about what I'd say and how I'd feel if someone kept telling me that. I too would probably think that they were lying to me. I once met a lady who just was flat-out stubborn. But I really feel that she had a mental illness more than Alzheimer's. I think she had a bit of both, but more of mental illness I'd say. I interviewed her on her condition and found that this lady was very clever and smart. I talked to her about Alzheimer's, and she was more than willing to talk to me. She started off by trying to put me in her seat, asking me how Alzheimer's feel and what these types of folks do. I laughed in my mind because I don't think she realized that I was interviewing her. She really laughed when I said to her, "No! I'm here to talk to you about your Alzheimer's." She laughed and laughed and said, "You think I have Alzheimer's? Ha-ha-ha!" She laughed and then said, "You're kidding me, right?" Maybe I shouldn't have, but I said, "No, ma'am, you have Alzheimer's." I asked her why she only has on one shoe, and she said, "Oh, the cat probably has it playing around here somewhere." But the thing was she had no cat. So as the interview went on, I decided to steer clear off that dreaded word Alzheimer's. She really hated it. I asked her who she trusted the most to make decisions on her behalf, and she said, "God." I was so surprised; she did have three kids. She then said, "I don't trust my kids. All they think of is money!" She had Alzheimer's and was beginning to forget everything, but she didn't forget God but forgot her children. That was so awesome. That confirms my suspicions of God's realness. He has the last say on all things, and that also showed me that we could not make it in this life without him. A lady with Alzheimer's didn't forget the Almighty and powerful, awesome God. Usually you might expect them to say something like "Who's he?" or "What's that?" But she had forgotten her children but not the Father of all of us.

"The fear of death follows from the fear of life. A man who lives fully is prepared to die at anytime" (Mark Twain).

Young versus Old

Now that I am a much older and wiser woman, I sit and look back on my life, good and bad, and try to figure, if I had the chance, what I would do over and better. And what I could come up with was not to had been so naive and thought a lot harder about some decisions I made about my life, not of been so free-handed, went after my dreams no matter who fed me negativity, although I believe that you can still accomplish your dreams at any age. For me it sure would have been a lot better for me to go after them at a younger age. But I still get the mental pleasure of knowing that I went after them at my age than none at all. I believe that the one tragic thing that could bring sadness to one is looking back on their life and thinking that they didn't even try to go after their dreams and realize now that they may be far too old to accomplish it. But I still say if you've got the motivation and drive at that older age, then you can still go for it. You can do it.

"The greatest robber of the mind besides Alzheimer's is having a dream and not going after it" (Brenda).

Older people bring a lot of wisdom to the world to share with those who are hungry for knowledge.

They have an advantage over the young by being able to place information in a meaningful content; they have the ability to use a greater number of words. They have greater supervising skills than the youth. They're far better equipped to read other motives and intentions while being patient and tolerant. Today's youth are all fingers, as I call them; because of new technology called the Internet or cyberspace, they can with one click of the mouse be anywhere they'd like at any time. Amazing, isn't it? That's the world we live in today. So if you're fifty and older, if you're not in the game, then you're struck out of it; and it will quickly move past you. I don't know if this new gift to the world is a gift or a curse. Some may say, "Is it really moving our world on to higher and better grounds? Are we in some way headed for destruction?" A lot of our elderly think it's ole Mr. Lucifer, the devil, or Satan. Either way it goes, our elderly I feel should not be left out of the picture. After all, this will someday be you. Ain't no escaping it. I don't care how many injections of Botox you may get or how many facelifts you have. You will still God willing live to be elderly. So enjoy your life as much as you possibly can. See as many new things as you can. Do as many new things as you can. Live your life.

Computers versus Caregivers

Now I've heard rumors of a possibility that computers may replace caregivers in the future. Now I really don't know what to think about that.

The jury is still out as far as I'm concerned. There may be many who will like this new concept. They say instead of a person who may be living in a nursing home, sitting all day watching television, and losing more of their mind. That maybe somehow the television could be turned into a computer and help support that person's mind. Fill it with activities instead of just staring at the walls. Now that thought in itself didn't sound too shallow to me. I'm all for helping someone keeping their mind intact. I surely couldn't imagine not having my mind. Now this may put a lot of caregivers out of work, and that in itself will probably start a lot of protesting. After all, a computer or robot can't really give the physical affection that humans can give: hugs, kisses, etc. What about changing soiled undergarments? Can a robot successfully do that job and leave the patient clean enough? I don't know what conversing would be like. This goes back to where I was speaking of our elderly learning about the Internet. Would an elderly person like having a robot care for them? I'm about half and half on this subject, but I strongly feel that having a real person may go a lot further. A lot of the elderly from my experience love to converse about the old days if they can. I don't really think a robot's conversation would be as real and as natural as a human's. One problem it may fix, though, is people showing up late for work. Robots will have the ability to go on and on without getting burned out. Well, that's unless they have some mechanical problem. But they will never be late for work, and if the facility is staffed with a great number, then there will always be someone on duty. But for me this proposal still has the jury out. I really think that a lot of folks will be against it, but who knows what will happen? Is this what our health care assistance is coming to? As I said before, it will help in a lot of ways where dependability goes, but I don't know how our elderly will feel. They are already used to years of having the human touch. I know we will have some who may feel this is a great idea, especially if they are being mistreated physically, and they'd also be grateful to getting attention anytime they'd like than waiting long periods of time for assistance because of staff being short, something I've dealt with while working in numerous facilities. There was always someone calling in sick. As I mentioned before mostly because of the type of residents we may have had, people with advanced Alzheimer's can be a big handful. What was supposed to be a part-time four-hour shift felt like eight to ten hours, and a regular eight-hour shift felt more like sixteen hours. You can sometimes be really put to the test. So again switching to robots may stop the burnout, but there are still other issues to be dealt with. What about the housekeeping issues or medication assistance? All this will need to be looked at. Humans make medication mistakes all the time. But will a robot make even more? What do you think? We really don't need our residents in any care facility getting the wrong medication. Who will be liable for the mistake if someone dies? The robot? I don't think the robot will have any fear about losing his job and not being able to provide for his family. They'll just wind up another and send him in. No, seriously now, I'm sure this will be some of the main concerns before anything is carved in stone. Touchy, touchy subject. I can't wait to see the day that this is broadcasted on your local news. Some will be frozen and can't speak, and some will had a hard time learning what it meant just like I did. This was just a piece of information I found in my research that shocked the hell out of me, and if you are a caregiver reading this, it may shock you too.

If I Had Alzheimer's

As I've worked with so many folks with Alzheimer's, I often wondered what it would be like to have it myself. When I'm caring for someone, I catch myself staring at them and really deeply concentrating on them wondering what are they thinking, what they are forgetting today. I sometimes find myself truly getting upset because I feel that because I'm always around them, I will get it, but I know better than anyone that this is not a disease that is contagious. I think because of all the sadness that's all around me all the time, it kinda got me down. But I really get right back into it because it's my passion, and I love knowing that I helped someone who couldn't help themselves. If I had Alzheimer's, I think I would probably be very nice but at the same time try to get things to go my way. As I am right now, I don't like to depend on others unless it's absolutely necessary and there are no other options. I'm a bit stubborn that way. I probably would have a problem with sharing a room with someone else since I love my privacy. Sharing bathing facilities would also be a problem, depending on how clean one would be. I would get thrown out of the kitchen most days. I'm sure I would be walking around in the kitchen trying to find out who's cooking what. Now this would be in the beginning stages where I'm still a little aware of my surroundings and who's who. Even though I'd have this disease, I would probably still try to help the others who have Alzheimer's as long as I was able. As I look at these ladies and gents who have this disease, my heart cries for them. I sometimes think it's gotta be so tough. But I think that the tough part may only be in the beginning. As I said, when you've still got some memory going on, I think pretty much after that they don't really realize anything much as far as being close to anyone, and I feel that is what makes this whole transition sometimes easy for these folks. After all, recollection of anyone close or in the immediate family is gone; it's probably a feeling that you have no relatives, and you were pretty much here all the time by yourself. Well, that's what I feel it would be like. I'm sure someone else has another view of it. I have a little girl who has more experience with people with Alzheimer's than me. She has been on many live-in jobs with me, and she had earned the respect of a caregiver. She is such an inspiration to me and these folks. They loved her everywhere we went. She automatically had that sense of love and care for someone. If she'd see a walker starting to roll, she was right there. If someone needed help standing up or a drink of water, my little sweetheart was right there. I would just like to give a high-five and hugs and kisses to her for all her hard work. She'd often have a question like "Mom, isn't there anything we could do to try to make these people's brain work better again?" Then she'd say, "I have an idea. We can raise money, and if we get enough, maybe the doctors can find a way." This is coming from a five-year-old. I'd tell her, "Sweetheart, I wish it was that easy. I really do." And I'd watch as tears welled up in her little eyes. She really wholeheartedly felt for these folks who really weren't a relative or someone she really knew. She is just a little girl with a big heart. I've met so many negative people who have said to me, "Yuck, how do you change those old folks' poopy diapers, and how do you put up with all that running up and down?" I just tell them it's my calling, and it doesn't bother me one bit. I always try to reiterate to people if it could be them one day, wouldn't they want someone to help them? That usually quiets down the subject totally.

It gives them something to think about. You don't know what's around the corner for you. People can be so cruel without ever thinking. Just because your horse is still in the race doesn't mean he's gonna win, honey. I've even had other caregivers who were supposed to be sharing a shift with me nearly vomit when they saw me help someone with their undergarments, and they were there for the same reason but spent their whole day complaining of how gross it was. I'd look at them and say, "Why did you take this type of job?" And most of them would say, "Oh, girl, I'm just here till something else comes along." And all I could think was "So you really don't give a damn about these folks. So selfish, so childish, and most of all so disrespectful. Where's the integrity, the grace, and the love?" These types need to have jobs shoveling slop. I'm sorry, that really kicked me in the gut. What are you really here for?

Kids and Alzheimer's

Kids can be good with a person who has Alzheimer's since most Alzheimer's patients convert back to childhood. They seem to get along well. Most children find it to be okay when they notice the changes in Grandma or Grandpa. At least I've seen that in the younger kids ages five to ten years. Most teenagers seem to take it a little harder since they are older and can see and understand some of the symptoms better. Most teenagers seem to have the most problems when the grandparents don't remember them anymore. They seem to take that the hardest. And I'm sure most people would take this the hardest. All of a sudden, Mom can't remember you; not even your voice lets her know you are her child. Sometimes the grandparent may become combative, and this really hurts if that child would get yelled at or even hit by their grandmother who normally didn't have a mean bone in her. We must let the grandchild know that it's okay to be afraid and assure them that it's not the grandparent's fault. It's only the disease. So when they are talking to that grandparent, they should just go with the flow and don't try to figure out anything or question them over and over with the same question. They will never be able to follow your conversation or answer any of your questions correctly if they are in more advanced stages of Alzheimer's. Just enjoy the time spent with each other. Kids can make something to remember their grandparents. Try videotaping fun times you had with them while they were here. Make a scrapbook together if they are able to help. Make as many memories and take plenty of photos before the disease gets very bad. You will always be able to look back at the good times you did get a chance to share together. I once knew of a little lady whose great-grandchild came with the parents to visit, and he would always sit on his (nana's) grandma's lap and kiss her right on her cheek. Most times she would usually just smile and give him a hug. After a few months went by, the grandma's Alzheimer's had progressed; and when the grandchild came over, she was really mean and would no longer allow her grandson to sit on her lap. She had completely forgotten him and could not recollect anything about him. This broke his little heart, so they no longer brought him along on any more visits. What bothered me was that the granddaughter had gotten secretly angry at her grandmother for the harsh treatment of her little boy. And I thought I made sure that she understood this was to be expected after all the conversations about changes that at some time would occur. You can't take it personally. She said crying, "Oh, I'm sorry." It just hurts to see her treat her baby like that, and it was hard for her to get over that. Soon I noticed that her visits had gotten shorter and shorter until she stopped visiting completely. She stayed away until her grandma passed away. She held a grudge all that time simply because she chose to take it personally. I guess as long as it wasn't harmful to her child, she could take it, but the grandma never acted out physically. She just wouldn't have anything to do with the grandchild any longer; she would no longer allow the child on her lap. We are all sensitive about our children, but in this case, the mother should have been a little more understanding. She needed to understand like she told me she did. I carefully explained the changes that were to come. And she still didn't want to understand this. Again and again, I say you can't take it personally. People with Alzheimer's change all the time; you never know what you're gonna get.

The Rain

I stepped outside. The sun was shining so beautifully.

It reminded me of the flowers you once brought to me.

But that was oh so long ago. I'm so, so sorry. I don't remember anymore. After the sun soon came the rain. I started to feel I wasn't the same.

I saw your face, and my mind couldn't place what your name was. Had it been erased? Please forgive me if I seem a bit far. Know that I will love you like a distant star.

Hold on to our memories of yesteryear. Please don't cry or shed a tear.

For I will hold you in my heart always, my dear. We will walk through the rain without fear. As time goes on, you will slowly disappear but hold on to my memory. It's very near.

Chapter 7

Questions

I noticed when people usually converse with people who have Alzheimer's, they seem to forget that these patients are no longer able to hold a lengthy conversation. Most are only able to take in a few words at a time. Talking to them for long periods of time only will leave them confused; some may even get a little agitated and angry. Also, I've seen lots of arguing with their mom or dad who has Alzheimer's. It's a no-win situation. Believe me, you will end up getting so agitated that you will start to think you've got Alzheimer's. Some days they are up spirited and on other days down, not wanting to be bothered at all. This was all from my caring experience. Some may or may not have experienced this. But my guess would be that most have. Always treat your loved one with respect. Don't treat them as if they are a child. If they didn't have Alzheimer's, you wouldn't. Sometimes there will be an exception to the rule, and this will usually be when they are in mid to last stages. They can become quiet combative and use bad words to get their meaning across. When you are taking your loved one out for the day or out for a dinner, always be prepared for things that may stress you out; and if they are using undergarments, make sure you always carry extras in your car. Accidents seem to frequently happen. A fresh pair of clothes would be a good idea also. You may be out at the mall or somewhere and run into friends who haven't seen them for some time and are not aware of them having the Alzheimer's disease. So to keep all out of shock and maybe some shame, secretly let the friend know of the disease if you can at that time. You never want to use that word (Alzheimer's) in their presence, especially if they are still capable of understanding some of your conversations. This would be very scary for them and leave them confused as to what has happened to him or her. Always try to fill in words for them when they are talking and can't seem to put their words in the right form. But remember to give them a chance to try as much as they can then jump in when you notice the confusion coming in. Listen to them when they try to express themselves to you. Look them in the eyes so they will know that you care, and they have your full attention, and you are not just shaking your head. Take your time with them. They cannot speak or move around as fast as you're able to. So be patient. It's really good if your loved one is living at home to keep their world as quiet and as simplified as you possibly can. Make absolute sure that their room is clutter free. Just a few basic wash-and-wear clothing. Keep the nicer things in your bedroom closet if possible, dresser, bed, TV, if they still show interest, or music, a small radio is good. I've found most folks with Alzheimer's love music. Classical is good or what some of us describe as elevator music. Some even like gospel. Any good positive music is good.

An Early Grave

There once was a lady named Pam. Pam at the age of seventy-five had beginning stages of Alzheimer's. She would always want to talk to me about the disease. She was about the only one I know of with this disease that had the questions she had. She'd always say she is going to an early grave and how it wasn't fair because she hadn't finished living or following through with her life plans. When I asked what some of those plans were, she said one was to go to the Grand Canyon, and I said, "Well, maybe you can still get that chance. Maybe we should mention that to your children. Who knows you may get that trip?" As we talked more and more, I said to myself, "Wow, this lady doesn't need to be in a care home yet. She still has a great deal of her memory past and present pretty sharp." We went on talking. I told her of how I had a dream of going to Paris one day and stay in one of the best hotels and be pampered with a full body massage. After that, I'll go to a great live show at some theater and have a great dinner in one of the finest restaurants. She then said that would be good. She said she had plans to see Elvis on stage next week, but she thought all tickets were sold out. What's going on here? Elvis? He's been dead for years. What is she talking about? So I said, "Elvis? Didn't you know he was deceased?" She said, "No, Elvis isn't dead." She had seen him on the news talking about his upcoming show. I then said to myself, "Okay, I see some long-term memory kicking in here. She still believes Elvis lives." I finally convinced her that he was dead but not to worry because she wasn't the only one who believes he still is alive. But for some reason, I thought that she still believed that he lives but just didn't want to speak of it anymore. She went on to ask me how many years she had to live. I just simply told her to not worry about how much longer she would be on this earth but just focus on how much life she has in her now and to enjoy it as much as she could. I went on to tell her no one knows what tomorrow holds. We are here sitting and talking, but tomorrow could be my last day. I hope I get to live for many, many years to come. But in all reality, none of us really know when we will leave here. You're just more afraid because a doctor told you your time was short, but that could be for any one of us. The only difference is that we don't know. We haven't had anyone tell us our time is short. Put your trust in God and let him do the rest I told her. Then she said, "Who's he?" That was confirmation that she did have this disease with bouts of good memory popping up sometimes. Although we'd talked about what life has to offer, she still seemed to be very afraid and concentrating on the negative no matter how much I on a daily basis tried to encourage her. Although I didn't have Alzheimer's,

I think that I could almost feel what she was feeling; and the fear must have been overwhelming for her, not knowing when your mind will totally quit on you. No longer remembering your relatives or what your own name is must be terribly terrifying and unimaginable for those of us not aware of this disease nor have experienced it with anyone who has it.

When I Was a Little Girl/Boy

When you were young, just a little girl/boy, you all had dreams of growing up and one day to be a doctor, lawyer, pilot, actor or actress, or even Peter Pan. The point is that we've all had childhood dreams of being someone famous or someone special and greatly respected. I wanted to be several things: an actress in all the best movies and a surgeon. I loved to pick splinters out of other's hurt fingers. I loved to give care to others. It gave me pleasure to ensure that others were all right. I wanted to be a famous dancer and even a mortician. What a list. Have you ever thought or wished that there was a way you could fast-forward your life to actually see what you will become and then rewind it all the way back and change or take out the parts you don't like? No one probably ever fast-forward or rewinding saw themselves being severely sick or disabled. Why? It's unimaginable. Our minds just can't tune in to those kinds of realities, but we are so quick to realize ourselves wealthy with lots of money and all the finer things life has to offer.

Amazing, isn't it? I bet none of you ever imagined your mom, dad, or friend who you hung out with in high school, who would meet you someday at the same university, and the two of you always shared your dreams with each other. Your dream for your life. Then you hear that your favorite buddy or girlfriend who you were in college with years back can't remember you anymore because they've been diagnosed with Alzheimer's disease, and you really don't know exactly what that is. You heard the word thrown around here and there, but you still don't know what it is, so you go see your friend who you thought would be older now with their own family practice in one of the best parts of town, living a great life. But then they can't remember who you are when you finally go to see them. They walk right past you. You are a stranger. You're in disbelief and denial. How can this be? Just how quickly that incident took place? That's how quickly Alzheimer's can go through a family's life and turn it upside down. I wish there was a way that the first discovery of your pal or girlfriend having this disease could be easier, but there isn't. The harsh reality of it is it is what it is, and I bet it was never a thought in your dreams, child or adult. Life has lots of straight roads and turns. And you'll never know when that straight road will take a turn. A lot of us grew up and did live out our dreams, but it seems to be only a few out of the gang that hung out in high school way back when. Some of us did take that wrong turn down the wrong road. We experimented with drugs and liked it. Some of us had burning desires to be all we could be if only we had a little encouragement. Some of us just went for it all and got what we said we would just by being around the right people. Some of us were very successful but were stopped right in our tracks. Some of us got Alzheimer's and could never look back.

The Ghost

Someone once told me that they felt like Alzheimer's was a little ghost sitting on their shoulder tormenting them daily. This particular lady said she felt afraid and alone most of the time. She was fairly known with getting Alzheimer's. She was in the early stages. I must say it broke my heart. When I asked her what she was so afraid of, she said it was not knowing what was to come. I asked her to just focus on the now and maybe the fear may leave. She says every day she could feel a part of herself leaving, and that is what scares her so much, wondering when the day would come when total memory loss would come for her. Forgetting herself and her family, she said, frightened her so. She told me she started out putting notes up everywhere in her bedroom, on the lamp shades, on the bathroom mirrors, and on the refrigerator door. She then went on to say, as I listened with tears in my eyes, she found that she started to forget where she put the notes that she depended on so much to get her through the day. As we continued to talk, I could notice in her conversation her words were starting to sound muttered. I made sure I kept the conversation's speech slow so that she would not feel confused and lost. She said she didn't want to go to a home. She's heard so many bad things about them. I told her that she should have her family take time to pick a very good home for her, if and when that time came. They may just continue to have a caregiver at her home, which I thought was a great idea as long as she could be cared for there. This lady seemed to be very much still intact mentally; she could still write and read the daily news, although some parts were confusing and she'd stop right there. She was still pretty good in the kitchen as long as there was standby assistance. She served herself, cleaned up after herself, and put the dishes away. I discovered as long as a person was there keeping her busy, she was pretty much calm and not so afraid of the little ghost that had been around for some time. I told her it was time for the ghost to be put to rest for good, and as long as I was there, we would have good times and focus on fun times each day. That seemed to work pretty well for her for a while, although the ghost did try to come around from time to time. She in the end did have to enter an assisted-living facility and then on to a nursing facility with twenty-four-hour care. That ole ghost just seems to want to hang around and bother her day in and day out. Before saying good-bye to her, I asked that the staff keep her as busy as they could, hoping this would at least keep the ghost away part of the time.

Searching for My Mind

David spent most of his days fighting with everyone else who he said caused him to lose his mind; he spent most of his days trying to figure out where he went wrong or what medication the doctor had given him that caused him to get Alzheimer's, which he was in strong denial about. He always said someone or the doctor must have slipped him the wrong pills, and now his memory is slipping. No matter how it was explained to him about his diagnosis, David still was hung up on the fear that he was set up and tricked into taking meds that took his memory. He spent his days from beginning to end searching for what he no longer remembered. Every person in this adult family home had conspired in some way to take away his memory. To know David is to love him, although this may look as if this man could be a mean man. He was very soft-spoken and really showed strong expressions on his face with lots of serious concern that he was sincere about getting to the truth about his memory. I have met and cared for many different types of folks, but I think Dave was in a class by himself. Yes, he was funny at times and could still your heart with his big blue eyes. It's sad at the same time because I knew that he had Alzheimer's, but there was no way that anyone was going to convince this man that he was stricken with one of the most feared diseases out there. Poor fella. I sometimes wanted to hold him like a newborn babe. I tell him that it was gonna be all right to see him spend his days and on through till bedtime searching for his memory, or the person responsible for his condition was so heartbreaking for me. Sometimes, I wanted to somehow convince him that it was Alzheimer's and that there was no way that anyone could have stolen his mind. But there is no possible way to express or try to explain anything to someone with this disease—here in a split second, gone that fast. You may as well be talking to a stop sign. You have those big letters STOP looking at you right in the face, yet you still try to explain that it can't be done. I sometimes feel sorry for the relatives of those who have this disease; they somewhat go through a denial period too. They really think for a period that their loved one will come out of this. But the sad reality is there's no coming back.

The Face in the Mirror

Sadie wanted to know who the lady in the mirror was. That's not someone she knew or now remembers as Alzheimer's quickly moved through the many rooms of her mind. She thought sometimes the woman she saw was her sister or mother. As I worked with the many different personalities of Alzheimer's, one thing I found was pretty much the same. Some seem to recognize the face in the mirror as a deceased relative or a sister or mother but not themselves. This really baffled me, so I thought, *How could that be? How could I not remember even myself?* At that point, I really realized that this disease is really much more tragic than I thought. Can you imagine looking into the mirror and no longer knowing who was looking back at you? I can remember a time in my life when I couldn't even have a mirror in my bedroom because when I got up to go to the bathroom at night, I'd swear I saw a strange face looking back at me. This went on for a couple of years or so before I decided I'd either cover it up at night or have no mirror in my room at all. After scaring myself half to death one night and running into the wall, leaving a big knot on my head, I decided the mirror had to go and eventually realized that it was only me letting my mind imagine things. I wonder if that's what Alzheimer's does. Does it play tricks with the mind? I found in my research that most people with this disease are somewhat mentally ill also. Is that why Sadie didn't recognize her own face or no longer knew that face she had seen in the mirror all her life and knew who was looking back at her? When I went into the bathroom to wash her up one day, I said, "Look at that beauty looking back at you in the mirror." Instead of smiling, which I had hoped to accomplish, her expression became very sad; and she dropped her head as almost being ashamed to look at the person looking back at her. I asked, "Sadie, what's the matter? Why the sad face? Look at that beauty in that mirror." She quickly said, "That's my mother." And she quickly went out the door, almost as if she was afraid of what she had seen. What I wondered was, *Was that her mother in her eyes who had been deceased for years and years in that mirror? Was she in some sort of spirit world that we are unaware of?* It's baffling for me. I've taken many different people into the bathroom to give baths or just to assist them and would tell them to look at their beautiful self so they could feel good about seeing their selves after a shower or bath, and most folks seemed to like it and smile. I think besides Sadie, there may have been one or two who didn't seem to like it at all. I just wonder what really goes through their mind. Does this disease cause horrible hallucination in some? Your guess may be better than mine, or maybe Sadie hated her mother.

Am I a Walking Time Bomb?

People with Alzheimer's probably feel as though they are a walking time bomb. Just imagine if you can. Each day a little more and more of you is slowly slipping away. One day, it may be the memory of where the car was last parked; the next day, you forget how to put your socks on. Then all of a sudden, there's a big loss: you can't remember your name and then the names of others. It's just like a bomb waiting to go off. You're waiting for the last tick to tick, and then there's no more. Now that's only an example or feeling I got from someone who has this disease and was also very afraid. She said she felt like a walking time bomb. Each day a part of her body was melting away again and again until the last bit of memory had been taken away. She said she had dreams of being pulled left to right. And the being or people pulling her didn't have faces; it was as though they were just empty spirits.

Like a hooded man, when you really thought you'd see a face, there was nothing but air there. That's how she said she felt inside: almost empty. A little more going every day. It must be so painful to feel that way every day, fighting a fight that really can't be won. But I wonder, *Does that register in the mind of someone with this disease, or do they go on through the rest of their life feeling that they will be cured?* I suppose many really may just stay in denial and never let go because it's all that they really have to hold on to, a belief that there is a cure and that they will be saved right in time. I feel that if it was me in that situation, I would probably be in denial too, thinking that before I got any worse, someone would find a cure and save the rest of my memory. And as stubborn as I am, I probably wouldn't even believe the doctor when he told me I had Alzheimer's. I'd just figure he didn't know what it was and gave me a diagnosis because he didn't know. There are those kinds of things really happening. Some folks hang around for quite some time with this disease, and others seem to go pretty fast. Now statistics say one thing about the length of life with Alzheimer's, and real-life experiences say something more. When it gets down to it, I don't think anyone can really say how long one can live.

Fear of Speaking

I've noticed that a lot of people with newly diagnosed Alzheimer's don't like to talk too much or too long. And I've had some tell me it's the fear of saying the wrong thing or not making any sense or others secretly laughing or disrespecting them in ways like over talking them or cutting them completely out of the conversation. So they'd rather not say anything. But I guess either way they sometimes get judged if they say something or not. If they just stand there, some may think there is something wrong with them, but they don't know what. But I say, "Who really cares what they think? Your life is not based on their thoughts." I guess you can say that I'm a little sensitive about people making fun of or calling people with this disease names. Believe me, I've seen and heard it plenty of times through my journey. People can be so cruel. They didn't ask for this disease, so no one should make any kind of efforts to belittle or make them feel unimportant. It just boils my blood to see them being mistreated. Life's so short. Be careful who you treat badly. They just may be an angel. Wouldn't you feel bad if somehow you could really find out that they were? You may even feel afraid. After all, you'd be messing with one of God's greatest. I'd watch so many hateful caregivers just doing a job, treating folks so ugly sometimes, someone that could be their parent; but they couldn't see that far. I can truly say that through my journey, I've had lots of fun times with some of the folks. We've laughed so many evenings after dinner. We've cried together and found laughter in that after all. These were my children, once an adult now a child. My memories of some will forever be engraved in my heart. And some were just like saying good-bye to my biological grandma or mother. That's how close we became, and it was so sad to say good-bye. So if you meet someone with this awful disease, be nice to them and make them feel special. Speak slowly so that they can understand you and take the time to listen to them even if it may take them a little longer to finish their sentences. They really feel good about themselves when they feel you are listening to them. They feel that they are still a part of the normal life and the same as you and me.

Memories

Betty—she said she could feel the memories of yesteryear. They were at the tip of her tongue, ready to drip off and be lost forever. How the words she wanted to say were right there and in an instant gone, not to return. She often would try to recollect what it was she wanted to say, but just like water dripping into a pond, it slowly floated away. Oh, how frustrating she told me it was; it aggravated her soul. When her family would sit around speaking of old times, she felt her every word, anxious and ready to join in. But in a split second, it was gone. Her mind was telling her, "Hurry, hurry, get it out. You know it won't be there long." But her mind was not fast enough to keep up with everyone else. Oh, how she felt the excitement of remembering her late husband's birthday and wanted to join in and tell all about the fun and laughter there was at the party. But here again the speed in her mind couldn't catch up. She said her mind held so many memories, and she wished she could somehow store just the most pleasant and fun times in a different place, somewhere where the Alzheimer's could not erase it. I told her I would help her store those memories where they couldn't be forgotten or erased. I would have her daughter buy a recording device, and we would all sit down over lunch one day and help her take her back to the old days; that way she could listen and have memories all the time whenever she felt like laughing and remembering her husband's birthday party. Betty was very talkative before the Alzheimer's came into her life. She told me it felt like every time she went to speak out, it was like something just tied her tongue down so words couldn't be formed. I felt so sad for her. It must have been a fight inside that went on every day but was always a losing battle. She often liked to talk about her childhood and her school years; these memories seemed to still be fresh in her mind. It seemed to really make her happy to go back to her childhood and to have someone really wanting to take the time to listen to her. That made her feel normal again, if only for one hour. She could tell stories of her childhood so accurately and parts about her young adult life. But the present was like a whole new world someone had picked her up and dropped her off in. She said she never thought that she would be experiencing memory loss so severely at this time in her life, but there it was. I told her, "Oh, Betty, don't feel so bad. I'm not near your age. Sometimes I can't find my keys, and if I look long enough, I will find them in the refrigerator. So don't feel alone. Mine takes a leap sometimes too." And we both laughed. I'm sure that that made her feel better, and her day went a lot easier.

I Want to Be Held

Lilly was a very tiny little lady who I thought was sweet as sugar. Although she had Alzheimer's, there wasn't a bad word ever coming out of her mouth. Some with this disease become really combative and mouthy, if you know what I mean, but not Lilly. She was about ninety pounds and approximately five feet tall or shorter and about ninety years young. Lilly literally was like a little baby. She couldn't walk very well because of her back problems, so a lot of the time I found myself carrying her to the bathroom and things like that. Lilly would always tell me how she just wanted to be held all the time, and she was very aware that she had Alzheimer's and had no quarrels about talking about it. As a matter of fact, it was a daily conversation with her. She often told me that she was scared and wanted someone to be close to her at all times. She really had no family, just a sister who resided in a nursing home. Lilly would often tell me of how she wishes she could just hide out under covers with another human being and just stay there for the rest of her time. I often would try to encourage Lilly that there was nothing to be afraid of and that whenever she needed a hug, I was available and would even sit and hug her the whole time when we could watch a movie together. This really made her feel safe, I tell ya. She was like a real-life baby doll but much older. She often spoke of her younger sibling who she hadn't seen in a year because of the fact that she had health issues and couldn't leave the nursing home she lived in. I'd have to say Lilly requested a lot of my time, but at this particular care home, my time had to be shared with many others. Although Lilly had been spoiled by me, I made sure she understood that there were others there that would like to get the same treatment too. This made Lilly very jealous. When I asked her why she was so afraid, she said that she just felt that one day the Alzheimer's will just come and in one breath take her away. I'd try to convince her that I was sure it wouldn't happen that way and that she would have all her friends in the home, including me, all around her when that time came. And that all she needed to do right at that time was to focus on having lots of fun and good times with everyone there with her. Lillian was so afraid of this disease that she wanted me to sit by her even during meals. Now some have said Lilly just wanted to have me to herself; but no, I have to say she really truly was afraid, almost to the point that Alzheimer's was a monster that was really physically going to come in the night and take her away. I have to tell ya, everyone reacted differently with this disease, and the most popular one for me would be the fear, especially when no family was available. Lilly passed away a couple of months later, but I made sure that her last days were filled with laughter and joy.

In the Middle of the Night

I wake up in the middle of the night, tears streaming down my face.

I often think if I can win this race. I wipe the tears. I try to get back to sleep.

But my weary mind won't rest. It's weak. I reach out into the night, asking, "Dear Lord, help me win this fight." I get no answer. Are you there? Is there anyone out there who even cares? Loneliness rubs each and every bone.

This is where Alzheimer's has made its new home. Why oh why did you have to choose me? Please let me go. I want to be free. My memory, my name, my children, all melting away. I can't even tell them they cannot stay. Vigorously I search in my mind a cure; a solution, I try to find.

Where did you come from? I want you to go. I don't want to know you anymore. You've stolen my soul, the very part of me that strengthens my heart, each and every beat. I tried to ignore you when you came around.

But you were tougher than me, no chance I have found. Please allow me just one more date, an outing with my family. It would be so great. Just for a day, can I please use my mind and talk to everybody, like old times? Just time to remember each and everyone's face. Would you please spare me a little grace? To see their smiles and remember a face, just one more dance with my favorite mate. When I'm done, peace will take me to a place where there will be no more tears, no more fears, no more sorrow, through the years. In the middle of the night, I will rest assured that an angel from heaven came down like God said he would.

Chapter 8

Residence Inside of Me

I once spoke to a gentleman who said that he felt as if someone were living inside of him. At the time, I didn't think that this person had Alzheimer's. I really thought that he had a mental illness. All his conversations were about someone literally taking up a living space inside his body. I never cared for this person each day alone—there were many others who needed to be cared for—but I noticed that he had most of the same habits others with Alzheimer's had, you know, putting on three pairs of socks and three shirts, hoarding things in his bedroom, etc. On the days I did get a little free time just to talk to him, I found that what he was really talking about was the Alzheimer's taking over his body, his mind, and his speech, not knowing anyone any longer or even something as small as tying his shoes. I've taken care of people with mental illness, and most of them would tell stories of someone else living with them or seeing people in their rooms or bed. But this fellow was really dealing with a harsh bout of fear every day, walking around confused and wondering when his last day was going to come. I noticed that others working at the facility were talking of how he was up at night and thinking of getting a medication for sleep for him. As I continued to talk to him, the more I learned he was actually trying to see if by being up at night and day, he could somehow stop the Alzheimer's from coming in and taking his soul. Poor fellow, I thought, the things that must be going through his mind must be so scary for him. Can you imagine? Well, I can, since I had a long experience with fear. It's a terrible thing to live that way. Although I knew that there was nothing I could really do or tell him to put his mind and body at ease, I could maybe talk to him and calm him, if just for a while. People see and treat this Mr. Alzheimer's just like a monster of some kind, and I'm sure that's probably how it feels to some— feeling fear, anger, sorrow, depression, loneliness, and a big gulp of confusion day in and day out. It must be a monster within itself to deal with. All I could do was recommend a doctor to write him a prescription for anxiety meds to calm him a little. There was nothing more I could do except pray, and sometimes that can be the best medicine of all. After he received his medication, life for him had gotten a little calmer and a little brighter. I know it did for me. This man was no relative, not really even a friend. But he was a person dealing and struggling with an emotion unseen by others, and dealing with such a thing day in and day out alone must have just been horrible for him. I just happen to be one out of the many working at this facility that could somewhat relate to how he must have been feeling whether it's Alzheimer's, dementia, or anxiety from working overtime at the job. We all go through something that may put fear in us, and we too may search for a way to find peace.

Have You Ever Wondered?

Have any of you ever sat and wondered what day and time it would be when you take your final breath on this earth? Well, maybe I'm about the only one. I used to sit and wonder what day, what time, what I will be doing, and at what age I would be when my time is done here on this earth. I finally concluded that if I pass away in a hospital, I will have a pretty good guess about all my thoughts. It may or may not be exact. But I will be pretty darn close to knowing. I once cared for a lady who had dementia; her mind was still pretty much intact, though she couldn't remember often. She could hold a decent conversation and do a lot for herself still. She often talked about when she would die. She said to me, "So this is how I'm gonna die, huh, losing my mind, and eventually not remembering my own name." And then she would cry, and I'd console her and tell her it will be all right, thinking quietly in my mind, *Yes, that is a horrible way to go.* But then people have died in ways more traumatic, I told her, and that would be my fear—to be suffering and in massive pain all the time until my last breath. I don't want to suffer. I'd also tell her that the end is up to the Almighty no matter what man says. It's his call how and when you will leave this world. That seemed to always make her feel better. Death and dying always seemed to be a fascination of mine. I once applied at Gupton-Jones School in Georgia to be a mortician, and at some point, I decided I didn't want to. I still have regrets because I'm still fascinated by it. Even volunteer work in a morgue would be good for my interest in death. But somehow I still just never got to it. I've seen a lot of death and dying in my life, and it never seems to make me really sad. Well, that's unless it's someone close to me. But the very thought of touching the dead—feeling and seeing the difference between a live body and one that's just still, with no life, no emotion, almost like an mannequin, just a lifeless body, no longer able to laugh, or cry, or move in any way—always just seemed to capture my interest so much. I've been called weird. But if there wasn't anyone that liked this type of work or had interest in it, we would be living in a world full of corpses and no one to help bury or put away all the dead people. So as this lady told me of her fear each day of the dementia that her doctor told her would eventually turn into Alzheimer's, I said to myself, *Does it really have to go that far? Couldn't it just stop right there and just be dementia?* I'm no doctor, but I just wonder if there is someone who has just stopped right at dementia after being diagnosed with dementia turning into Alzheimer's. I told this poor soul not to put more into this disease than there needs to be. Doctors make mistakes all the time. Maybe her condition will just kind of simmer right where it is and not go any further and not become Alzheimer's at all. You know, hope is a wonderful thing. It can erase a lot of thoughts that were negative and replace them with peace where there once was nothing but weariness and sadness.

She Went Traveling

A woman in her seventies went traveling one summer. It took her days and days to get to where she was going. She stopped at a restaurant each time she became hungry and refueled her stomach and then got back on her journey. She saw many different things while on her trip. She saw old friends she hadn't seen in years; she saw places she had once traveled before. She saw lots of beautiful flowers and plants. She tried on clothing that she had once tried on before. She even saw an old boyfriend whom she had broken up with years previous. She saw things that reminded her of her childhood. Oh, how they cheered her so. Some things were so wonderful she didn't want to let them go. But she moved on. There was so much more to see. She was so excited, and she felt so free. It had been a long time since she traveled alone. She told me she was trying to get back home. I asked if she was moving away someday. She said she didn't know. She may stay away. As I looked at her, I decided to travel by her side. I asked this lonely lady if she needed a ride. She said, "Yeah, I'm getting a bit tired on my feet. I need some rest now. Tomorrow I'll do a repeat. That was a long hot travel for her that summer day." You see, she has Alzheimer's and was traveling across the way from the front yard to the back, at least twenty times per day. Her Alzheimer's mind took her along the way to a faraway place only across the yard. But in her mind, it was very far. Although I didn't tell her, I let her adventure be. She was on a vacation where her mind was free, back to the days before her mind was gone, back to the days when there was so much fun. Before Alzheimer's came her way, she traveled with her husband each and every day. Her search to find those wonderful days gave her peace in another place, a place where tears were not to be found, a place that was safe with all her old friends around. I told her I'd take the next trip if it's okay. She said, "Sure, you're invited, but you mustn't stay. I've reserved this trip for my special friends, and one day I may even see my husband again. So please forgive me." She started to say, "I'm not being rude. This has to be this way." I told her, "No problem. I respect your right to spend the whole summer with your husband this night."

Screaming in My Head

"Can you hear that?" she said. "No, Mrs. Parker, I didn't. What did you hear?" "Listen, listen, you hear it." "No, sorry, I don't hear anything," I told her. Mrs. Parker was a sixty-eight-year-old lady with Alzheimer's and who also suffered from schizophrenia. She often heard people talking to her and chasing her, which was so intense sometimes that it ultimately cost me my job. I quit not only because of frustration but also because of fear, fear from some of the stories she would tell me and the things that she saw. Sometimes we would be sitting watching a show, and all of a sudden, she would say, "Get outta here. We didn't invite you to sit and watch this program with us." I really wasn't too scared. Besides, I didn't see anything. But what would end up getting me was when I asked her what this person or people looked like. She would describe the most horrible-looking faces I wondered how she even slept at night. Since I had to be there at night a lot, I really started to wonder if there were really spirits there in the home. According to her, they were at the dinner table, watching her take a shower, picking food outta her plate at dinner. You name it—they were just some bad little spirits. And the expressions she had on her face were so real and convincing you didn't really know what to believe. So I decided I'd pull her doctor to the side and ask a few questions when she had a next appointment. When the appointment did come, I found a minute or two to ask him. He assuredly told me that it was all in her head and not to fear or let her get me rattled. That was easy for him to say; he didn't have to spend his nights with her. What did it for me was when one night I was asleep on the couch, and she came running out of her bedroom, screaming that a lady was sitting in her chair in her bedroom and wouldn't leave. She had a hole where her eye used to be. Then she said, "Would you please come get her out of there?" I had to go back with her to turn the light on to show her that there was no lady in her room. But little did I know the trick was being played on me. Before I could get my hand in the door to turn the light on, she pushed me in the dark room and slammed the door shut. You probably know what was going through my mind: where is the lady with the hole where her eye should be? And I'm the type that doesn't want to sleep in pitch darkness. There has to be a night light somewhere. After yelling about four times for her to open the door, she opened it with her hand over her mouth laughing. It was so funny to her. I was still shaking like I was freezing to death.

That was it. I was outta there. I had to stay the rest of the night up, drinking coffee to stay awake. No way was I going to sleep after that. Finally, she was asleep, but I wasn't taking any chances after that. To make a long story short, that's how that job ended with a relative of hers who came to relieve me unwillingly. I still wonder if this lady had Alzheimer's at all; she seemed to really get a kick out of scaring me more than anything else. But I must say I'm not that easy to scare, but she got me.

Terror in New York

The year was about 1981. I was living in Brooklyn, New York. At that time, I was caring for an elderly man. I can't remember his name. But he was at the tender age of ninety. This nice young man had a good heart; besides me, he had a caregiver who was his grandson. Each morning from Monday to Friday, I came in and cared for this nice man, getting him up out of bed, washing him up, and then preparing him for breakfast and morning meds. I enjoyed taking care of this sweet ole fellow. He was such a nice man to talk to and help with his daily living skills. After serving him his dinner, I'd wash up the dishes and get his pajamas on for bed. I'd make sure he was tucked in and safe before leaving. One and a half hours later, the grandson was due to come in and sleep over till the next morning. This was a pretty good job, except the grandson used a very abusive language to his grandfather. He would often ask the grandfather for money, and the grandfather often refused. This is when the grandson would cuss and use lots of profanity to the grandfather. Most times I never said a thing, but after the grandson left, I would always tell the grandfather to get rid of him and that he didn't have to put up with that abuse. This abuse happened quite often, but the grandfather would always just say he'd take care of it. Sometimes I'd notice a bruise on the grandfather's arm or neck. I was sure it was probably something the grandson did when he couldn't get any money. I felt so sorry for this frail man. He probably weighed no more than one hundred pounds and stands at about five to six feet. He was pretty skinny and sickly. The grandson was basically a bully. I really hated to see him come. He seemed to always be upset about life in general. I decided I would have to report him. On this day, he was very verbally abusive toward the grandfather; he really wanted cash very badly. I think he probably had a drug addiction to something. This is why he always seemed to need cash. He called the grandfather every name in the book. He was just furious about not getting the money. He stormed out, calling the grandfather a son of a you know what and how he hated him and he was gonna pay. I asked the grandfather if he wanted me to call the police. He said no and that he would call the family members to keep him out of his home. So I said okay and to call them immediately. I ended up working a few hours longer before going home, making sure the grandfather was safe. When morning came, I went back over to the home and let myself in. While walking through the home, I yelled for him as I always did, letting him know I was in the house; and usually he would call back, "Okay, I'm awake." But not this morning. I heard nothing. I pretty much knew he was gone. As I approached his bedroom, he wasn't in bed; so I headed for the bathroom, calling out to him, thinking he just may be using it.

After calling out twice and getting no answer, I decided to just enter the bathroom. When I did, I found him in the bathtub in his PJs, underwater. I grabbed him to try to pull him out, but it was evident that he had been there all night. My first thought was his grandson came back sometime in the night and murdered his grandfather for money. He didn't really like him anyway. I was the one to give him his baths. He would have never attempted to take a bath alone, and besides, the bathtub was full and running over. Who fills their tub to the very top like that? At least I know I don't. He was fully dressed in his PJs. I wasn't there to see it, but I knew in my heart that the grandson was responsible for this sad, sad scene. I told the police what I thought. All I know is that they questioned the grandson but never found out the outcome. This was such a heartbreaking end for this sweet ole man. Too bad that his own relative would kill his elderly granddad for money. I've seen a lot of greed in caring for different elderly folk but nothing quite as bad as that. This poor ole guy lost his life because he refused to give away his few dollars that he kept around the home for emergencies. That was years ago, but till this day, that job still crosses my mind. A lot of our elderly people are really being abused out there and in more ways than one. And the sad thing about it is it usually gets overlooked or just looked at as he or she was old. A lot of the time, they may have been secretly murdered; and the murderer got away with it simply because the person was old, and, oh, they probably fell. No one really takes the time to fully investigate. People never really put themselves in that person's place. That could have been you or your grandparent. You never know.

Interviewed before Memories Were Lost

I interviewed a lady once about the effects of Alzheimer's. Was it a little at a time like I had seen most of my caregiving years? Or was it rapid in some? I had witnessed that probably once or twice. This particular lady told me she tries to go to private places in her mind to entertain herself, but she finds that the sweet recollections are leaving, and it gets harder and harder to remember what she had for dinner the day before. She said how this frightened her, and it was almost like going under water and holding your breath for as long as you could and finally having to let go because that was as long as it could be held. She said she often thought as she went to bed each night if she remembers even getting into bed the next day, night, what time it was, and so on; and if she did, she'd know that the Alzheimer's was not moving through her as quickly. If she didn't remember, she'd become afraid because she then knew that soon, very soon, she wouldn't remember those that she loved. That frightened her most. She spoke of how her dreams were so very different than they had been in past months. They were more like she was in a different place, in a different time, and she was someone else with a totally different life. Sometimes she said she'd lie in bed and hope to drift back into that dream so she could be taken away from the reality of having Alzheimer's if only for one hour. I must say this broke my heart, and I told her that for me, if I had Alzheimer's, I would feel like pieces of my mind would be stolen bit by bit until the last bit had vanished. But I knew that I couldn't begin to compare or even come close to imagining what she must be experiencing. She spoke of how the fondest memories were the ones that seem to be drifting away quickest; and she often found herself, if she really focused, trying to retrieve those that are so important to her. Then the frustration of not being able to grasp them makes her so angry. She realizes that she has to move past that and focus on the memories that are freshest in her mind and try to hold on to them for as long as possible. To me it almost seemed like a race against time. You're racing to get to your thoughts before something or someone else takes it away, and you've gotta get there first. I guess this is why I do this type of work, and it is work. But it quickly can become very emotional and dear to your heart. As you care for these different folks, over the years, they become family; at least this is how it felt for me. There was no way I could see myself not getting emotionally tied to these folks. You care for them each and every day, talk to them, cry with them; and it sometimes feel as if this was your mother or father that you were caring for. And when it came time for them to pass away, you grew sad, and you start to realize parts of you went with them, and your heart is left just as broken as anyone else who has gone through the memory loss, the reminding, the leading, and guiding through the day and night, and the constant reminding of who you are. There were times when I felt as if I was getting Alzheimer's. Sometimes I got so closely involved that I found myself sometimes acting and doing some of the same things they did on a daily basis. I'd often stop and search and test myself to ensure that I wasn't getting memory loss because of overexhaustion of working long hours, repeating the same things day in and day out, sometimes bringing someone or keeping someone inside when they spend their days trying to leave the home going to a place they feel they are more familiar with, from times long, long ago.

Safe, Clean Eating

I've worked with so many different caregivers in my life. I always tried to remain professional with every job I worked, making sure that my experience with clients was memorable not only for them but also for myself. One of my biggest concerns and hurts were how new caregivers would come into a job that had been going great; and then all of the sudden, everything changes and most times for the worse, especially if you have a wonderful routine going already. Everyone has to share the chores and try to keep things in order as they were. But sometimes you get that one caregiver that comes in and wants to try to change the whole program and mess things up for everyone. Everyone had to share the cooking of what was on the menu most times. I encountered a caregiver who absolutely was not going to play by the rules. I am very strict when it comes to handling my food and how it's prepared and who's preparing it. And I surely expected the same when it came to the people I was caring for. This particular caregiver did not practice universal precautions or any precautions if you asked me: never washing her hands, never washing before preparing meals, and never washing up after coming from the bathroom, which eventually caused us to have a big blow-up. I'm a pretty bold person, and I was in charge, so I'd always kindly tell the other caregivers to make sure they'd wash their hands before leaving the bathroom. I felt I had to remind the new one in particular constantly because factually I knew that she wasn't washing at all. She'd come straight out of the bathroom and into the kitchen and proceed to the refrigerator. This is where I had to always intervene. She would drop food on the floor and say, "Oops, it's still good," a five-second countdown or something like that. In other words, if you pick up the food off the floor, no matter how dirty it is in five seconds, it was still good enough to eat or cook. Not in my book. If she herself wanted to eat it, fine, but don't feed this to the residents we were caring for. That made me furious. She just refused to abide by the rules and was let go. But I could not believe how many people are working out there, mishandling the food we eat, and yes, I must burst this bubble. Nursing homes and some private care facilities have this habit pretty badly. There are plenty out there that I wouldn't feed my dog out of, let alone a human being. This is why lots of people get sick, and sometimes the doctor doesn't know why. I will be willing to bet most times it's from someone being unsanitary with the handling of food or even cooking outdated old food for the sake of trying to save a penny. I decided on giving up most restaurant food, especially fast food joints.

I will not even begin to start on them. Be careful out there. You never really know what you're eating unless you cook it yourself, and that's always the best way.

I'm Tired

I'm so tired of all the private care homes and nursing homes that let the resident lie around all day in wet undergarments. Yes, this happens; so if anyone out there says "That doesn't happen here," well, good, I hope it doesn't happen where you are. But there are plenty of places out there where it does. A lot of facilities don't enforce upon the caregivers enough to change or at least check their residents' undergarments at least each two hours at a minimum. I've seen so many bed sores, skin breakdowns, and rashes because residents aren't getting checked on or changed regularly. It saddens me to see an older mom or someone's dad lying in their own urine or feces all day long with no one coming to change them. Oh, yuck! As if your s—t doesn't stink too. That's what you're there for. You already knew beforehand that you were going to be changing soiled undergarments and cleaning lots of backsides. That's the profession you chose. I know someone informed you about this at the interview. So enough already with yuck and "Ooou wee, it smells." So does your child; so does yours. The children of these ladies and gents are expecting this from you. That's why they placed them there in your loving care. I've seen so many bed sores I can't begin to count. It often makes me wonder if our health care system doesn't get something in place to stop the abuse and misuse of our elderly's funds. I'm fearful that it could be waiting for me or people I love and care for. These folks pay a lot, expecting a great return in getting great care from caregivers and those in the nursing field. Meanwhile, a great majority are just getting pushed through the system.

As I Look Around

I used to visit nursing homes on a regular basis. I'd go and hand out flowers to people who I really didn't know. But just seeing people lined up along the corridors of these facilities would really make me sad. They're lined up as if they were getting ready to go through the assembly line for their meals. A lot of them didn't have relatives that came to see them, so somehow I felt I had to fill in for those who had no one just to put a smile on their face. Loneliness is such a sad, sad thing. I often put myself in their place, which seemed easy to do, because this really concerned me even if these folks were no relation to me. They always looked so sad when I came through. A lot of them were slumped over sleeping, and some of those who had dementia or something were often reaching out as if to say, "Come talk to me." I always had a strong desire to become a nursing home administrator. But somehow I got much more pleasure doing direct care, talking with these folks each day, caring for them, just putting hope and a smile on their faces.

Anyway, if I were an administrator, I probably would have been so strict that the staff may have bonded together to get rid of me. I think giving care was my calling at that time. I enjoyed it and was great at it. Hopefully, by the time I need someone to care for me, I'll hopefully be one hundred, and God will be my caregiver like he is today. If not, I hope he'll bless me to be still in my own home, which I'm sure a lot of folks wished they could have been. So many memories at home, so many familiar things, family photos, the smell of familiar food cooking, and the smiling faces of your relatives—that's the best show in town, I think.

I'm Still Alive

"I may have Alzheimer's," she said, "but I'm still alive. I still can feel what it's like to kiss someone. My heart still flutters when I kiss the one I love. I still have feelings just like everyone does." There was a little lady named Clara and a man named Bill. Clara loved the ground Bill walked on. She'd follow Bill around the world if she had to, although I think that Clara liked Bill a little more than he liked her. Bill had a wife that came to visit him regularly, and Clara would burst a bubble when Bill's wife would kiss him hello and good-bye. Through my journeys, I've seen a lot of ladies pursue men when they were in the middle stages of Alzheimer's. It often puzzled me, you know, even though they had this awful disease, they didn't forget how to love. I've seen women fight over men and have even seen some try to take over and become very angry when the wives came to visit their husbands. They'd sit in the corners hugging and kissing, holding hands, and even lying in the bed together. This disease has so many sad and bad effects, but somehow these folks didn't forget how to be affectionate. Most of the time, they are usually fighting over silly little things or busy getting into something. It's so amazing how this disease affects some people differently, but the majority have the same actions and do mostly the same things. I once took care of a young lady who was mentally challenged, and she had a boyfriend and ended up getting pregnant. Now this was in a group home for the mentally challenged. To me, that was not a good situation, especially at the level of care needs for these two people; but the owner of that facility says they could not stop them from being sexually active. I really thought that would be somewhat against the law, but according to that group home owner, they couldn't do anything but let the social workers and family handle it. I really thought that was something. But I guess that goes back to their rights, and they are still people just like you and me. The only difference is their challenges were a little different than most of us. They were two very nice young people; they had part-time jobs at some of the local Salvation Army and St. Vincent de Paul stores, so they were pretty high functioning. I never found out how that situation ended. But what I'm trying to say is these folks remember these emotions and love to be hugged and kissed. At least most of them do. So we must be kind and understanding to these folks. They aren't really that different when we talk about their spirit, and that's something we all have.

CHAPTER 9

Stuck in a Dream

I once took care of a man who led a very busy life. He was in charge of a lot of aircraft. Although he had Alzheimer's, as far as he was concerned, he was still flying. He'd get up each morning preparing to go to his office and start his day. There were days I'd have to try to redirect him and get his mind tuned into something else. Sometimes it worked, and sometimes it didn't. He was a rather charming and very tall man. I always really went along with what he was usually saying unless he really started to act out and try to leave the home when playtime was over, and you'd really have to redirect as quickly as you could. Some really, really believed it was forty years before and that they were actually going to their old place of employment. Sometimes they could really become combative about the situation, and oftentimes it would be hard to calm them down. It's amazing what they can and cannot remember. I know it must be hard to be replaced in your mind by something you're not familiar with or even know. This man was very busy in his working days and had several others working under him. So he was busy giving directions, and that's why he sometimes directed me. Most times I'd go along with him until he got uptight and really was going to leave the house. As I said, he was a big tall man, and when he became combative, it was hard to calm him down. But most times he'd listen. I've had others that flat out would leave the home, and I'd have to go running behind them to bring them back. They were usually going back home to a place they used to live before they had to be placed in a care home. Most times, when they were running away from the home, they were really in the advanced stages of Alzheimer's; all memories of family and friends were gone. But somehow they did remember that they lived in their own place before. One person worked all her days as a teacher, and she was always running to get the books together so the children could study from them. I remember her walking around the home, collecting all the magazines she could find, and setting things up at the table so her students could work and set up at their desk. When they came in, she'd actually sit and teach them math, etc. It was so funny to me how she'd be able to take a magazine that may have clothing in it and make believe that there were math problems in them, and she couldn't figure the problems out herself, but she was going to teach her students. It's baffling how they can remember about themselves forty years ago but not what's going on right now.

A Shock

When I was a little girl, I never ever thought that I would grow up to care for elderly folk and love it. I always thought I'd end up being what I always said and thought about: an actress or model. Do any of us really do what we say we are going to do or be what we say we are going to be? It hurts me to see that most of my friends who grew up with me said they were gonna be doctors, lawyers, police officers. It's funny how most of them ended up being locked up by the police and calling the lawyer to get them out of jail, and the only doctors they saw were the ones that tried to save their lives you see because most of them died young because of hard drug use or something along those lines. Life is so funny. You can never tell what will be waiting for you around the corner. I feel really blessed to still be here when my closest friends are all gone now, and I was blessed later in life to give birth to a sweet little girl whom I simply adore. She's my BFF for real! It's also funny how some of my older friends and people who I thought would be healthy and around for quite some time ended up with Alzheimer's, and even their own children never thought something like that would ever, ever happen. I once knew a very classy lady. I couldn't imagine seeing her any other way except for how I remember her: classy, stylish, with integrity, and beautiful. She got Alzheimer's, and life as she knew it was flushed quietly down the toilet—no more diamonds and pearls, no more brand-named or tailor-made clothing, and all the best places to eat are all gone. Now it was wash and wear, no more beauty shop for hair appointments. I looked at this beautiful person because beautiful she still was. She no longer knew anyone or what a brand-named outfit was or what to have her nails done was. As a matter of fact, she'd really get upset if you attempted to polish her nails or even put lipstick on her. Her mind had totally forgotten everything that was somewhat mandatory to her everyday dress wear. This lady now only wore sweatshirts and a gym pants, sneakers, and disposable underwear. The change in her features alone was amazing; even though she was still beautiful, you could see that there was no more light in her eyes. They almost looked deeply saddened and confused. It's pitiful how Alzheimer's can strip the very life from someone whose soul is still alive. Some looked dazed and confused and sometimes in a trance or hypnotized. I think the initial discovery that you have this disease leaves you totally lost until acceptance or total memory loss sets in, whichever comes first. Then in my opinion, you probably thought that things were always that way.

Getting Use to Dying

How do you get used to dying? Personally, someone that hasn't gotten any notice about death and dying, I guess you'd say it's nothing for me to get used to. But for those who are facing death, it could probably be a daily horrifying experience. I guess I would be emotionally a mess and physically in the fetal position every day. That's until I finally found acceptance with it all. I think anyone would have to come to acceptance first before they could mentally deal with the fact that they are going to die. I spent time with a lady who was worried all the time about dying from Alzheimer's. I couldn't blame her, but she was in the very beginning stages and really had a few good years in front of her before all the ugly parts of Alzheimer's set in. I think that she was more worried about the fact that soon she wouldn't remember her children, herself, or anyone she loved. My heart really went out to this lady. I knew that she must have been flooded with fear. This thing was new to her, and she didn't really know what to expect. No one really expressed to her what she would be experiencing. So I told her what I knew and tried to make her feel better about some of the changes she would be going through, although she was still a little frightened, and that was to be expected. It would probably be long after she's into middle stages of Alzheimer's before all the fear calms down a lot more. Alzheimer's has many faces, and most of them are scary and depressing. I know that most folks really become deeply depressed at first. Then all the other faces of Alzheimer's will finally make themselves known. Family and outings for as long as you possibly can will be very helpful in keeping the mind going and focused on other things. Parks and zoos can be good places to go to, as well as lunches out of the home. Just being around loved ones and staying busy can really redirect the mind if only for a short time.

Talking in My Head

This nice lady loved to talk, and just like me, I knew what she meant. I love to talk too, so I decided to put some of it down on paper. She often told me that she felt as if each time she started to talk, in her mind, she was chasing the words down or trying to catch them so she could put together a sentence. But the race was a steady, ongoing, never-ending battle for her. It must have been such a tiring, stressful thing to chase after something you could really never catch up with. Sometimes she was very quiet around friends and family. When I asked her why she didn't feel like talking to her family, she said she was trying to jump in the whole time sorting through the words trying to form a sentence. All she seemed to be able to put together was mumbling. And she felt she'd just get embarrassed if everyone saw that she couldn't form her words. My heart really went out to her. She was such a sweet little lady. I often told her Alzheimer's was a real little bugger but just try to enjoy the rest of her days as much as she could because it's not over till the big guy upstairs says so. He can make and change anything. I told her not to focus on the Alzheimer's and just focus on her family and take every minute she could to enjoy them. She often said the words ran through her mind like a race; she could visually see them like a little train running down the tracks reaching out to catch them. Only her hands were moving in slow motion. Most days she said it captured her soul. She was so overwhelmed with it all that it was the only thing she had room for. It must feel like she was in some type of prison. Only her mind had been captured. All the effects from Alzheimer's to those of us who don't know much about it, it's probably unimaginable to even think about; do you know that it could be knocking at your door, and in your family as fast as you can say Alzheimer's, especially if you have a family history. Statistics show that it could be passed on to other family members, and then again, it will simply pass up other relatives.

Wishing Me Well

A lot of folks with Alzheimer's do not like to be hugged or want you to sympathize with them. They don't seem to want anyone feeling sorry for them. I think they are frightened because of the constant reminding and people sometimes talking to them as if they are not there. I even had someone tell me that it was so aggravating for friends and relatives feeling sorrow for them, and they're not even in their graves yet. So this becomes a constant reminder of the disease they have. I know that if it were me, I wouldn't want everyone to feel sorry for every turn I took. I would like to be treated as normal as I can for a long as I could as long as I was clearly speaking when I was talking and everyone could understand me. They could just save all the kinder words when that final time came: my funeral. Most folks with Alzheimer's don't like to take baths either. It's something to do with the water I think. I think that the water's spraying on their skin somehow scares them. I had so many challenges trying to give baths to folks I've cared for. I've had some folks fight me and take off running in the nude to get away from the water. Then I'd have to chase them to get their clothing on or a robe or something. It's always best to take a tiny break and then try again later. It must be just awful to be afraid of the basic habits of life—things we do on a daily basis—and then not to even know or recognize them anymore. For me, not being able to talk would probably send me to Nutsville since I just love to talk and I know I can go on for hours. I once worked for a care provider who didn't think anything of her residents not getting a bath. She thought it would save on her water bill and laundry. I thought, "What an awful person." I then wondered if she even washed her own butt. I can remember once when she got angry because I wanted to give a bath to a lady before bedtime so she would sleep well. "Oh," she said, "if they don't want a bath, I don't give them one." I then told her, "But this lady wants to take a bath, and I better get it in before she changes her mind." They change like the wind. Some days are easy, and some are all-day challenges. But you somehow get through it all one minute at a time.

Beating Death

"Each and every day I find myself trying to beat death, trying to hurry through, and do all the things my mind tells me I won't get to," she said. "It seems the more I try to catch my mind, my dreams, the faster they run. I need to store them away for later," she said, not realizing that later will never come for retrieving her most precious memories. So she found herself running faster in her mind, chasing the things that were still attainable if she'd only hurry, desperate to collect the most precious things we all value so much. This lady had tried to race against time to try to keep them when us with a normal mind have a daily opportunity of turning off and on the things we want to remember, and off again when we don't. For someone with Alzheimer's, it's a constant battle of the mind to hold on to a thought that is there for a split second and lost among pebbles in a pile of one million. She said she wish she had a rewind button, so when she got closer to her time to leave this world, she could simply touch the rewind button and review and enjoy all the fun and precious memories of yesterday, if only for a while, a little while. As I watched the tears well up in her sad eyes, I thought to myself, *The world that she lives in must be a land where sorrow constantly resides and fear is always at home.* The home that her mind used to know has long ago moved away. There will be no coming back; there will be no more moving back in, no more unpacking and starting over again. It's all over, never to return again. Can I go as deep as she to even simply try to see this through her eyes? And then I realized I can only go as far as the caregiver, see this through the caregiver's eyes. And sometimes it can be just as much sorrow and sadness for the caregiver too. Although the caregiver may not physically feel the mental anguish, she can see and have an experience that's almost as close as being right there inside that place where this lady is visited each and every day.

Shall We Have Tea?

She was left alone and decided to have a cup of tea. As she put the kettle on and waited, her mind quickly drifted away. She noticed that there was a whistling noise coming from somewhere in the house but didn't know where it was coming from. She walked around and around the house, trying to find the whistling noise, and finally discovered that it was coming from the kitchen stovetop. As she grabbed the kettle, deciding to make herself a cup of tea, she realized that she didn't know what her next move was to be and also forgot to turn the burner off. Staring at the kettle, trying to figure it out, she tried anxiously to retrieve in her mind why the kettle was there in the first place. She knew it was for some reason, but what? After rolling this around in her mind for a while, she decided it was no longer important and didn't get to have her cup of tea. Staring out the window, she knew something was really going wrong with her mind, but what was it? She couldn't figure that out either. Then the fear set in from one extreme to another. She didn't know what to do. "Am I going crazy? Should I call my sister or take myself to the doctor?" Had someone already told her about what was going wrong with her? "No, I'm just overreacting. Calm down, and order in my mind will soon reappear." After resting for a while, she decided that she would try to have another cup of tea; but again, she still could not figure out how to get the burner back on. After messing around again and again, she decided finally that she wouldn't get the tea until her sister returned home. After her sister told me this story, I couldn't believe what I was hearing. I told her that she had put her sister in a very serious position that would bring harm or even death to herself. A fire or any serious thing could have taken place that day. I also told her that I think it was time for her sister to have a caregiver, at least part-time, but the sister insisted that her sister was capable to be on her own. I then asked if I could come for a visit to meet the sister. After meeting her, I could clearly see that she needed an in-home caregiver right away. Or one day she would be coming home to a home that had been burned down with her sister inside. That was just a tragedy waiting to happen. I could somewhat see that she didn't take me seriously, and I never did find out the outcome of that situation. But I did know that that situation needed to be changed right away, or one day, she will meet her worst nightmare: her sister losing her life in a house fire, when something could have been done long ago, if only she could look at the situation with seriousness. I don't know if it was a money problem or what that situation was, but I did know that this lady had the beginning stages of Alzheimer's, and her sister really needed to address it ASAP.

Flesh-eating Alzheimer's

This wonderful lady that I had the chance to meet and interview told me that she felt as if she had the flesh-eating disease, but only it was Alzheimer's eating her from the inside out. Every day she said she felt as if Alzheimer's had taken another bite off a piece of her mind. It was slowly eating and biting off pieces of her brain at first, and it slowly was working its way down her body. She said it seemed to want to go back and forth between her mind and her speech. She sometimes felt she had no tongue because when she tried to speak, she often was tongue-tied and couldn't form her words. Unlike the flesh-eating disease, there was no physical pain felt; but there was pain, and it was in her heart, and it hurt almost as if something were taking bites out of her flesh. She said each morning as she awoke she had a feeling that something was missing and something had come in the night and had stolen another piece of her soul. She had lost most of her appetite, and she felt like that came from the Alzheimer's eating at and making her stomach nervous from all the worry about what would become of her. She sometimes wished that it would just all be over very soon; it would at least give her peace of mind instead of sitting and waiting for this disease to wipe her out piece by piece. That was more like a slow death and being tortured along the entire experience of it all. As she checks herself daily, she notices that there was something she wanted to say and remember for the next day; but in a blink of an eye, it was gone away, never to be retrieved. It would make her so sad. This flesh-eating Alzheimer's is much smarter than me, she'd say. It sneaks up on you when you least expect it. And before you know it, another thought is gone. Then the anger sets in. You want to pick a fight with this monster called Alzheimer's. You want to take it apart piece by piece with the hopes of destroying each and every part of it one piece at a time, so you'll know that you will never have to worry about it biting on you ever again. But then reality sets in, reminding you that this is one fight you cannot win. And if you try in the ways you think about in your mind, you will only inflict horrible pain on your flesh. So you take a step back and tell yourself you cannot win. This is the hand you're dealt, and you must deal with it as long as the dealer hands you the cards, and you say, "I'll find peace somewhere through all the misery, all the pain that's in my heart. Learn to take the good with the bad, and one day this long-dreaded fight will be over, and I will have peace."

She Wandered Away

She woke up one morning, and her mind had taken a turn. She got dressed and got into the car to go to work. She had forgotten that it had been several years since she had been employed. She started out on her drive something that was just as simple as riding a bicycle again. She made wrong turns down the wrong streets, almost running into other drivers on the road. As other cars honked their horns and yelled obscenities at her, she smiled and kept on her way, thinking that she must be late for work by now. As she continued to drive, she finally figured out that she was lost and didn't know where her job was or how to get there. As she went down the wrong way, more cars honked and yelled; finally, someone had called for the police. They quickly got to her, thinking she was some crazed maniac out to harm others with her horrible driving. When asked by the officer for her license and other credentials, she couldn't produce them because she didn't know what they meant. That's what she told the officers. By searching through her purse, all they could find was a pair of socks and a photo of her grandchild. After a thorough conversation with her, they could see that she was not on drugs or a crazed lady out to hurt others. She was able to tell them her address and the name of her husband who had been deceased for many years. Finally, they got in touch with her daughter who had to leave work and come to collect her mom. This really put fear and regret in her daughter. She really didn't think her mom would take the car, being that her Alzheimer's diagnosis was fairly new. She then knew that she had to come up with other plans to secure her mom's safety. They hired a caregiver who worked out great for their mom, and life for her was much easier. She was once again explained to about her not being employed. I was happy that things immediately got straightened out for this lady; unlike in the previous story, this daughter took her mother's situation seriously ASAP. Relatives sometimes stay in denial about their loved one's condition. They hate the fact so much that their loved one has this dreaded disease that they sometimes go about their daily lives ignoring the condition, hoping a reverse change will magically come along.

One More Dance

One more dance before I go, one more dance across the floor. Won't you take my hand, lead me to a ballroom dance? Swing me, turn me, hold my back. One more dance will be exactly the way I'd like to leave this beautiful world I will no longer need. When I'm gone, just think of me in that one last dance that made me free, free from all the horrible thoughts, things that I could have and the have-nots. As I stare into the chandelier, I feel such happiness. I feel such cheer. I no longer fear this Alzheimer's thing. One more dance, one more fling. No more dark days, no more dark nights. All I can see are the bright lights. One more dance. Won't you come dance with me? Swing me across the floor, fancy free. Peace of mind is what I'll have. I'll be so free, no longer mad. Mad about this disease that has come upon me, taking my mind, haunting me. Mixing me up and throwing me down, squeezing my face making me frown. So come on, come dance with me, come one, come all. Everyone that Alzheimer's has against the wall. Come feel the joy of finally feeling free. Come dance with me. Won't you feel fancy free? Touch of a hand, leading me to another place where everyone's full of glee. No more whispers about who I am. Just conversations of splendor and crowns. Come dance with me. Come all the way. Come go with me. You won't have to stay. I'm going to this place very far away where there's total peace and people always pray. One more dance to say good-bye. It's a celebration about the end of my life. The end is near, only in this place where God is taking me. I think I'll stay. In my new home, ooh, I'll find such peace. I find such comfort. I find what I'll need. As I take this one last dance, there's something that I want you to understand. Don't cry for me. Don't shed a tear. Hold me close to your heart. I'll always be near. So when you're dancing your last dance, think of me. Remember how we danced fancy free. Remember the bright lights, the beautiful chandelier. Remember our last dance. It was full of cheer.

Chapter 10

Don't Be Alone

Statistics show that the elderly live longer if they have a companion, like dogs, cats, gold fish to feed, something to attend to every day to keep them busy. Loneliness is a killer of the mind. It will sneak up on you like a thief in the night and eventually steal your soul. So if you have an elderly loved one who is able and living alone at home, don't forget about them. Go by sometime, bring them lunch, take them out for a walk, bring them that new dog or cat or goldfish if they don't already have one. It saddens me so to see an elderly person who doesn't have a friend. If you can even pick them up, take them to a senior center for activities if they are able to go. A lot of the elderly find that they have lived their lives, and often when they are depressed and the children are all gone away, suicide often travels through their minds. As the saying goes, use it or lose it. Or even better, get busy living or get busy dying, as the great Morgan Freeman once said. I always pictured myself when I'm older in front of my fireplace in the winter, drinking a cup of my favorite tea or hugging my grandchildren, if I get some, and still writing books as long as my mind will allow it. If you keep your mind active now, you will be able to use it for a long time later. So keep it busy, and it will last you a very long time. I take pride in helping our elderly. Don't you know you can't and will not be young forever? We all have to get wrinkles, age lines, and sagging skin. There is no escaping it, so get ready; and while you're on your way there, help an elderly person who will be grateful for you to come by and clean their home, go and get the groceries, or just come by for a chat. As I get older each year I discover something different about myself, whether it's on my physical body or something disappearing from my mind. We all get some parts of dementia at some point in our life, and it's only forgetfulness from getting older that does not lead to Alzheimer's.

Some of us aren't as lucky. We get a diagnosis from our doctor telling us we have dementia and that it soon will become Alzheimer's. So as a last thought, stay busy and active as long as you possibly can. Most importantly, keep your mind as involved in reading, writing, staying busy as much as you possibly can. You'll be glad you did.

Not Me

Can you imagine getting a call after getting a checkup from your doctor, and the nurse calls you to come back in because your test results say you have a serious ailment, and you will only last a year or so? Denial will set in first, and you'll say, "Not me. Those results just have got to be wrong." So you go back home and try to figure out why and when this happened to you. I can imagine that's about what it will feel like after getting a diagnosis of Alzheimer's. SCARY! No one can be prepared for a bad diagnosis. Most of us go on with our normal life each day without something like that even crossing our mind, and the reason why is that it wouldn't happen to us. That's always someone else's problem, not yours. But I'm sure many folks who have gotten a bad diagnosis said the same thing. What would you want to put in place before your memory left you after getting an Alzheimer's diagnosis? What would you want to say to your children before you forget who they are? Where would you like to travel to? This may sound a little silly, but what favorite dessert would you like to eat before you forget what it is? Or what favorite meal? I say this because some people that I've taken care of all of a sudden hated the taste of some of their favorite foods. Don't know why. No one knows what tomorrow will bring. I knew a lady that would absolutely not believe or accept that she has Alzheimer's. She'd nearly curse you out or strike out to even try to hit you. I know it was only the anger from getting the diagnosis of the disease and denial. She really knew she had it but was furious that she did. I couldn't blame her. I'd probably be the same way. That is one of the most feared diseases one would get. I would probably cry each day for a very long period before I accept it. Then I'd probably let go. None of us who don't even know what this disease is couldn't and wouldn't probably acknowledge it even if we knew someone who had it. I've been up close and personal for at least twenty-five years with this disease, so I've seen it through the caregiver's eyes. I've seen so many tears, so many fears, so much sadness through the years. So many aching hearts, so many trials, so much "I can't believe this, not for a little while." So if you happen to see someone with this disease, shake their hand and be for real please. Treat them kindly as if it were a friend. You never know you may see it again.

Mourning Your Own Memory

Can you imagine this? You know you're going to die but only the doctor has told you when or how soon. Every day you cry inside yourself about the day you'll be gone. Every little thing you think of hurts—your funeral, how many of your friends will be there—and you try to guess how many won't even come. You wonder about the pastor and friends saying their good-byes and what they liked about you when you were around. How you were so nice and how much fun you were. I once spoke to a lady about this; she didn't know the exact date. But she knew it would be soon. Just like us all, we know we are going to die, but we don't know the exact date. I guess it's a little scarier when a doctor has actually given you a certain amount of time. She told me of how she mourned and cried inside, how she wished she could be around for her great-grandchildren. She said she'd like to do a few fun things before leaving here.

But all her energies were focused on dying, and it was hard not to think of it; it consumed her entire mind and soul. She said she feared sleeping sometimes; also, she had the fear of not waking up. A lot of her sleep hours were spent thinking and preparing for that tragic day or night that would be her last. She thinks about all the holidays she wouldn't get to spend with family and all the Christmas presents she wouldn't be wrapping this time since Christmas was one of her favorite times of the year. She said it seemed that since her illness, she felt that no one wanted to spend any lengthy amount of time with her. So that made her fear that many wouldn't be at her funeral. I told her not to worry; she won't be aware of it anyway. And if I were her, I'd spend my last days enjoying the things that made me happy whatever that may be. I can somewhat imagine what she may be going through, although no one told me I was dying, but I know how being abandoned by those who claimed they loved me felt. Sometimes you can live your whole life and find out that the people you thought you knew well you really didn't know at all. Death is such a sad thing, knowing you'll never see the people you love again. Many folks that I've taken care of didn't have anyone—no family. And the fear of being alone when that time came frightened them so. I've comforted many who were alone. It was so, so sad to me I almost felt obligated to hold their hand or spend time cheering them up some if I had extra time to spare.

I'm sure none of us want to be alone when our time comes, but then some of us will not have a choice. Live each day as if it's your last. Some feel you've gotta have lots of money to do this. True, most things cost to enjoy the fine things in life; but what I have discovered is the smell of a flower and the way the leaves change from green to yellow to red and orange are just about the most beautiful things I have ever experienced, and they're free. Just open your eyes. There are lots of beauty on our earth that's wonderful and free. Make use of it. It's the small things that we tend to overlook that are really truly, finer, and all free.

Temptation When You're Dying

I once spoke with a lady who told me of all the things she was tempted to do before she died. She said she wanted to take a ride on a Ferris wheel at a carnival. I thought, *Okay, this is something where she's going back into her childhood,* or she just wanted to do that. Maybe she had never taken a ride on one. I didn't think to ask. Can you imagine? What would you be tempted to do if you were at the end of your life? Would you be tempted to do things that were very scary and you always feared, or would you just make a bucket list of all the things you want to do and try to do them? Well, I guess if you had

Alzheimer's, you would probably have to do them safely with someone, and I'm sure it would have to be at the beginning of your Alzheimer's, providing you enough memory about the experience. I could almost feel the desire and the anxiousness of this lady, knowing that she was dying and she just wanted to have a little fun before she passed away. It brought tears to my eyes. I just hoped that she could do a couple of the things that would make her happy. I hoped her family would do the honorable thing and let her see some of her dreams come true. If I were in her position, I would like to be able to live out some of my dreams. Only if I was able to understand it and do it with my two children. I think we all have a bucket list and would like to try to make sure we can experience some of the things we've always dreamed about doing. It would be great! This poor lady was so fearful that she wouldn't get to experience a Ferris wheel and die happy and unafraid that she spent a lot of her time sad. This is why I so hoped she'd get to do the things that were on her heart and leave this world happy and unafraid. Have you ever just sat down and thought about what it would be if you only had one week to live and if you could do just one thing to make yourself happy or experience the one thing that you never thought you could? What would it be? Well, I have. I don't know about you all, but I think like that all the time. (Well, I'm special.) But seriously, as you're sitting there reading my book. Afterward, if you can remember, think about it for a few minutes. What would you really choose to do? Whether you have Alzheimer's or you're just a regular happy and healthy person, what would you do? Hey, life is short. Enjoy!

A Dream I Had

I had a dream last night. It had me so uptight. I couldn't wait till it was over. I thought I was in a fight. I couldn't wait to tell my friends the next day. There was excitement within me. Could this be real? Should I pray? Oh, I was so afraid. Something was chasing me. Monsters and doctors and men with chains are running after me. "Wake me up," I said. "I don't want to be here anymore. Someone please help me shut this door." As I tossed and turned and rolled around, I realized it's just a dream. What do I do now? Could it be real? I'll ask my friends if I cannot remember then. Maybe this dream will come again. I can tell someone if my memory will allow. Someone told me I had something called dementia. I don't know what it is. I can't remember. When did this happen? Where did it begin? Is it something I could call a friend? Someone told me it was not my friend. It will bring other symptoms, one called Alzheimer's. It's the leader within. As I tried to express this dream to my friends, my memory got lost. It was gone again. This monster inside me seems to come along at night. He sneaks under my covers and starts a fight. He makes sure he's gone when I'm awake. He doesn't want others to know he's after my fate. Will he be waiting when I've gone back to sleep? Will he be watching when I start to weep? I had a dream I was lying on the beach. The sun was bright with sand on my feet. Why oh why can't I stay in this place, where my mind is free and there is no race? No race to see things I hadn't seen, places I haven't been, dreams I haven't dreamed. So they say it's dementia, or was it Alzheimer's? They said, "Either one." I know I will dread the people ignoring me, whispering, staring, and always assisting me. I long for the days when I was fancy free, living in my home with no mind games to bother me. I had a dream of long ago, a dream of love forevermore. One day, the one I love will come running my way, and I will tell Alzheimer's to go away. We will waltz through the night along the shores, and there will be no more bad dreams, just moonlight forevermore.

Simple Tasks

When you have Alzheimer's, things can be very challenging. Every simple task can be like climbing a mountain literally. Emily had forgotten to remember how to tie her shoes, and it almost took an hour before she just got the strings together to finally tie them without the bow. She forgot that she had already put her shirt on, so she had on three now. Can you imagine not knowing how to do a simple task like tying shoes or putting a fork into your mouth or remembering how many pairs of socks you put on? This is the everyday occurrences of those who have Alzheimer's. I say to myself when they are adding more layers of clothing or trying to figure out how to get a spoon into their mouth, *How much weight is that physically on their brain?* I wonder, *Does it really, really stress them out to try to figure things out?* You know where to put this, where to put that. Is that why some people with Alzheimer's become combative right out of nowhere? I just wonder. Simple things that are just regular take more energy than we can imagine. I'm no doctor, as I continually mention throughout my book, but it almost seems that one part of the brain is simply telling the other side to shut down, if you can understand what I mean. Things most of us take for granted are so precious for those with Alzheimer's to remember and those close to them that are their caregivers. Most of us go through life never giving the little things one thought. I guess we never would because it's not affecting us at the moment. That's the way the world rolls these days. Since it's not affecting me, it's not my problem. We can be so selfish, can't we? I'm thinking that each day maybe one thing at a time goes.

One day a person with Alzheimer's can do things, and the next, he or she can't remember just how to retrieve them. I know I cannot begin to imagine how they feel. I'm sure none of us can. I would compare it with a young child learning to tie their shoes, eat with a spoon, etc.—once and adult, twice a child. And I think that that goes for us all. But for those with Alzheimer's, it proves a lot worse.

Come Back, My Love

Myra was a ninety-year-old sweetheart who adored her deceased husband, Tom. Tom had been dead for thirty years or more. But in Myra's mind, he had just taken a trip and would be home very soon. Each day and night, Myra took her husband's photo everywhere with her, even to bed. I thought that this was the love story of all time. This lady had been married to this man for about fifty to sixty years, and he had been deceased roughly thirty years. This was a care home, and Myra didn't receive too much love from some of the caregivers because of the fact that the photo went with her to dinner, to shower—everywhere. I mean this lady simply adored her husband, and I saw nothing wrong with that at all, especially because I was in mourning about my husband too, except he wasn't deceased. I had just gone through a divorce, and in a way, it was just like going through a death. So it's somewhat harder to accept. Anyway, I could understand what Myra was going through. This lady did a lot of crying, which seemed to aggravate the other caregivers. But I kind of took her under my wing, and we somewhat consoled each other. I had to constantly tell her that her husband had gone on a six-month fishing trip. Before I came along, all she got was "Well, he's dead. Get over it." *Oh, how inconsiderate and uncaring,* I thought. This lady needed comforting ASAP. So I made her my project. I convinced her that her husband would be on that fishing boat for six months and then be on his way back to her.

This seemed to really work. She got involved in other things that took her mind off Tom so much. I also went and bought a teddy bear that was two to three feet tall and wore a hat. We decided to name him Tom. After a while, she was carrying this large bear around, but it was treated more like her husband, and she talked to the bear as if he were Tom, and the picture went back on her dresser where it belonged. She eventually forgot about Tom and the fishing trip, and the bear was still there to take his place until he returned, which she knew in her mind would be one day. No more hearing the caregivers telling her how her husband was deceased, hurting her more and more when in her mind that was just not true. So finding another focus for her really helped, and she knew she would see the man she loved again one day, and the teddy bear Tom made things easier for her. As for me, I just had to go through the normal grieving process and accept that the love of my life wouldn't be back, and I had to heal and go through this one day at a time. I was fine in the end. Maybe I should have gotten myself a teddy too.

Man in the Mirror

Murry had Alzheimer's. Each day Murry's routine was get up at 6:00 a.m., shower, and shave, then eat breakfast. Although he was in the very early stages of Alzheimer's, he still had a pretty good short-term memory. He even read the morning paper at times, fed his dog, and went for his morning walk. Most mornings, he found his way back home just fine, no problems. But on this morning, he had to stop three blocks from home to try to remember which way he had to go to get back home. After ten minutes of thought, he finally remembered which way he needed to go and returned home. Usually he would go with his wife, who was employed, but she didn't go on this morning. Since Murry had light Alzheimer's, he no longer worked. Around the home, Murry performed the duties his wife usually would perform, most things outside of cooking, though he could easily get himself lunch. The next day, when Murry went in to do his regular shave, he couldn't figure out where the shaving cream went and ended up putting it on the hair on his head; and this is where it remained until his wife came home, noticed it, and wondered what was in his hair, and he could not tell her. His Alzheimer's had jumped to a different level overnight, which in my opinion was very quickly. His wife decided to get help from an agency ASAP. Murry started to stop doing a lot of his regular routines, like walking. These things seemed to go very quickly too. Although Murry attempted to try to go into the bathroom to shave, he ended up standing there trying to figure out what he needed to do. Murry had totally forgotten how to shave himself. So he just stood there staring at himself, and this became a daily ritual for him. His wife and anyone else who tried had a hard time removing him from the mirror. I thought he may have been trying not to only figure out what he was doing there but also to determine who the man in the mirror was. Looking in the mirror every day for weeks, Murry had forgotten himself. It's so sad how Alzheimer's sneaks up so quickly like a thief in the night and robs a person of their most precious assets: their memory. That is something we all need and cherish, for without it, what and where would we be? It's so needed, and we have not even really thought about not having it until it starts to leave, and it usually starts giving us a problem around our forties. Well, speaking for myself, I noticed I started to forget around that age, it had me looking in the mirror too. Alzheimer's may come into your life one day. Let's hope not, but before it does, try to eat lots of brain foods. Try your local health food stores to find the right ones.

An Alzheimer's Prayer

Thank you, Lord, for blessing me. Today I was told I have Alzheimer's disease. They say it robs you of your mind. But I know with you I'll be just fine. They say I'll forget you and can't call on your name. I told them you're all-powerful and always the same. God, I'm asking you for this day. Please, dear Lord, take this devil away! The doctor said I won't remember you. I told him you're all-powerful you'll know what to do. He offered me pills, said they were the best for me. I told him your medicine has made history. My Lord, dear Jesus, I will always honor you. When I can't remember, I'll hand it all to you. Even though this may be your will, I will still go with your amazing skill. Your healing touch that can move a roaring sea, even with Alzheimer's, you can still heal me. There are many who doubt your mighty strong hand and ask why you do this to man. I tell them to not question the ruler of this world, for even if I have Alzheimer's, I'm still your girl. I'll always be a child for you, once an adult, twice a child. I will always follow you, even when my mind is all gone. I know that you will still have it and nothing will be wrong. So when my friends try to put blame on you, please give them comfort and rest in you. I try to figure this whole thing out. But I did hear your voice telling me you're here, no doubt. You said, "My child, do not be afraid, for I am the one from which you were made." Although others may not see me, I will make sure to give them peace. Hold on to my hand as I take you away, and do not fear. I'm here to stay. This world you leave was just a visiting place. I will now take you home to your rightful place. Tell your friends you will see them once again. You're going home with me. Shed no tears or sin. None will understand when you try to call their names. But I will give them peace, so do not be ashamed.

Amazed at Memory

Clara was a lady I took care of in Atlanta, Georgia. Clara had mild Alzheimer's, so she could still do things, like brush her own teeth, make a sandwich—the little things. One day while making lunch in the kitchen, Clara noticed that she made herself a sandwich without forgetting to put everything on it. Clara was so amazed that she thought her Alzheimer's was in remission. "Brenda," she said, "I think I'm going into remission. I'm really starting to remember things a lot more nowadays." I told Clara that Alzheimer's won't go into remission. At least I hadn't met anyone who had. Clara was a little stubborn, and no matter what I said, she was in remission as far as she was concerned. So what could I do? I let her believe what she wanted to believe; besides, it made her feel great. Alzheimer's to me is an ugly monster that sneaks up on a person, and at the last minute when you think all is fine, it steals your entire memory and leaves you empty, not remembering a thing about the person you once were. Imagine your entire mind disappearing in a minute without notice. One memory at a time, some days one or two things, other times half of your life in a few hours. It's amazing the power it has over your brain in an ugly kind of way. And what's worse is there is nothing you can do to regain something that is so precious to us all. You're watching television, and you see what's going on in front of you. But in a second, as quickly as looking away for a second, you cannot retrieve or even tell anyone what was just said or what had just happened or what you just saw. It's something, isn't it? Clara's mind finally did leave her bit by bit, piece by piece; and each day as I watched, I saw her eyes get sadder and sadder, and the light in them gets dimmer and dimmer. I often wondered if she somehow could remember thinking about what she said about being in remission, and I thought about it too. And my conclusion was no, she didn't remember that conversation. In the end, Mr. Alzheimer's took away another fine person. Clara was my friend, and I missed her very much. But I'm sure she's in heaven talking with God, and her memory has been restored.

Chapter 11

One Last Chance

Her mother died at the ripe ole age of ninety. Most of her life, she had no real relationship with her mom, well, not the usual type of relationship a mother and daughter should have. Now that she has been diagnosed with Alzheimer's, she wishes that she knew her as an adult. She had heard about all the awful things Alzheimer's turns you into. She became more and more afraid of her approaching the reality, which was unstoppable. Some days she wished her mom could be there so that she could lay her head in her lap and cry herself to sleep and feel a little better about the horrible disease that was slowly nibbling at her soul. She found herself getting all her ducks in a row by setting up her funeral arrangements and leaving some of her favorite things to some of her favorite friends and relatives. She wrote letters and left notes to people who she thought had made a difference in her life. She felt as if she had to cover each and every aspect and corner of her life before this dreadful disease took over the once sharp and orderly mind she was always so proud to use in helping others. *Oh,* she thought, *what would they think?* She now has Alzheimer's. What would people say about this woman who once could stop a crowd of people by speaking out loud about the things that interest most? The strength in her voice had no longer stood its ground; instead, it had turned into a calm meager little voice that could barely be heard or understood. Almost in shame, she dropped her head when she spoke because of the fear that people would whisper when she could no longer form the words in her brain so that they would make sense to others. She often privately wished that she could have one last chance to talk to all her old friends about the old days, days when they were young and life was simple and new and carefree. Just one last chance to slide down the sliding board, to swing on the swing, or ride around on the merry-go-round, as the wind blew through her hair, and she didn't have a care in the world. *Oh, how life was so sweet,* she thought, and that was something that she could never remember ever again, like most of us. Those sweet childhood memories will be gone forever for her and for others a treasure that would be carried through all the years of one's life. Oh, how sweet life could be without this dreaded disease. She finally decided to accept this thing she really had no power over and just hold on to the memories that were still present, and she could have that one last chance to remember the childhood days that would soon be gone forever.

Who Are You?

As he looked in the mirror at himself, he wondered if the man in that mirror was him or someone he knew. The tall skeleton-looking shell of a man he saw didn't resemble him at all. After all, he remembered himself as a handsome, well-nourished, well-built tall man. And the thin sad-looking man he saw scared him so. He started to wonder if this happened to him overnight. Had he been that way for a while? But he didn't realize because his memory at the time wouldn't allow him to know who he saw in the mirror. Left with nothing but total confusion, he wondered what he should do. Had he been to the doctor already? Did the doctor know about his shrinking thinning body? Does his family know and he had just forgotten? Or is everyone deceiving him and not telling him anything because they do not want to frighten him? He didn't really recognize himself. If it wasn't for him not being able to form a sentence that made sense, he would sit his wife down and have her explain about his weight loss if she knows. He noticed that she seemed distant and avoided lengthy conversations with him. He wondered about the time he has left to live. Why isn't anyone telling him or spending time with him? Instead, he spent most of his days staring out his bedroom window. Mealtimes seem to be the only time he spends any real time with someone he knows. And most of the time, that person is only his wife. *Where are his children?* he wondered. Had he forgotten their faces? Had they come to see him often, and he just cannot remember them any longer? He finally came to the realization that he had this awful disease that is taking over his soul. And the thin man he sees in the mirror each day is him. So he accepts his new fate and decides to live the rest of his life as happy as he could make himself. Life for him usually is the same thing day in and day out. His wife has a lot of cheerful conversations for him at dinnertime, which he thoroughly enjoys. But that seems to be the only time he gets anyone to talk with him. They don't realize how he craves conversation with those that he loves, especially his children who rarely come around anymore. He's afraid that they may not like seeing him as frail and thin as he has become, and this makes him very, very sad. So he goes through his life day by day expecting a change, a change that may never come. At least one thing has come true. He now knows who he is. For now, he has decided that he has today, and that's one day more that he can say he knows who he is. And Alzheimer's hasn't yet on this day stolen all his mind.

Open My Cage

As she sat there looking out the window, she could feel herself shaking her cage. "I can feel my arms reaching out to shake the bars that wouldn't budge. What do I do? I'm trapped. I'm trapped! Hey, help! Help me! Can anyone hear me? Oh, there is so much confusion and turmoil going on inside my brain. I need help to escape this cell of terror. I'm in prison. This disease I have has trapped my very soul. I can't think right. I can't eat right. My very speech has been attacked. Is this why none of you can hear me? They said it was Alzheimer's. Could this be what it is? If so, can't someone please take off these locks? I'm shaking this cage day after day. I yell for my mother, father, sister, and brother. And still no one appears. No one can hear what's going on except me. I'm the one fighting this battle, just me all alone. They can't hear what's going on inside my brain. Oh no, so no one will ever hear or feel the misery I'm living. No one will ever know the sadness I feel, the fear of death, the loneliness. I can remember a bright young lady with a bright wonderful future, a long life of things to expect like travel, dinners in fancy places, holidays like Christmas and Thanksgiving. There will be no more gift giving, no more eggnog. Whom will I serve? Will I be alone on these days because I will now be a nuisance to those who claim to love me? Oh, I want out of this cage," she said. "God, can you hear me? You're the ruler of all mankind. You have the power. Please open my cage. I don't want to live like this. Is this your will for my life? I have so many questions for you. I'm shaking my cage. I'm rattling my chains. Won't someone please try to hear me, PLEASE? As I sit here and think of these chains, I become angry. I want to break them, cut them off, only my strength won't allow me to. I have no more power. All my muscles are weak. I'm trapped in this cage. Oh, I'm so weak. I've been shaking my cage for some time now. I've finally found out that no one will ever come. I shall be rattling and shaking this cage for the rest of my days on this earth. If there is anyone out there shaking their chains too, please don't try to fight them or figure what you can do. Instead, relax and enjoy what you can and the people around you. Shaking your cage will only waste the rest of your time. Don't be like me, searching for something that won't be found."

As We Age

As we age, I think fear probably attacks most of us, especially those of us who have poor health and no reliable retirement fund at all. Imagine being the age of, say, sixty. You're five years away from what's supposed to be retirement for you. But you probably only worked two, at most, part-time short-term jobs in your entire life. You were never married, with no children or relatives you can really rely on. What do you do? Just think about that for a moment. (What do you do?) Well, I happen to have known some folks like that in my life. And they ended up like that at their own hands—being lazy, if I can be so bold. They spent their lives having fun, partying every day of their lives, with no Social Security coming—nothing, except maybe to get in line to hold up a sign on a street corner if they can find a spot. These days, every street corner you see has at least two people holding up signs. Even that occupation, as I call it, has gotten full. Now imagine being in this predicament, and you find out you have Alzheimer's. Wouldn't that be just the pits? I mean the scary, scary pits? Where would you go? You have no health insurance; your mind is slowly leaving you. Just what do you do? Welfare, huh? Again at today's rate, that will be nonexistent pretty soon. We are hearing so many cases of this disease daily that a lot of us may see this disease in our lifetime. And I feel the ones that will almost definitely see it will be those who do drugs on a regular basis or just recreationally. You see, you're already frying your brain cells. So how could you think that Alzheimer's couldn't be far behind? And that's just my view of the situation. The world we now know is changing at a very fast pace, and our resources are going right along behind it. Alzheimer's is a very trying and very miserable disease. Since I've been around it so much and have cared for so many afflicted with it, I can almost feel what some of these folks feel. Spending years up close and personal with them has given me plenty of insight on how these people must feel, so if you don't have it. But you can relate to what I was saying about not having anything going for you such as health insurance.

Even if you do have the insurance, it won't stop Alzheimer's. But at least if you do have some insurance, it can provide you the opportunity to get on medications that can slow this monster down. This is why this subject is so important to me. I don't have the disease. But I believe if we all work together, we can stop it from affecting many in this world in which we live.

A Cry

She could often hear someone crying. She never knew it was her that she heard crying until one day she looked in the mirror and realized it was her. She said she could always hear a lady crying in the distance but never gave it a thought that it could be her. *Why am I crying?* she thought. She finally figured it out that she was the one crying, and she knew something was wrong with her, but she didn't realize she had Alzheimer's. The crying was going on every day in her head, and this was why no one came to her aid when she cried out to them in her mind. This is why no one saw the tears streaming down her face. She was living in misery, day in and day out, screams of fear, tears of pain. Not physical pain but the pain of possibly losing her mind forever. What would she do? What could she do? Who could she tell? She realized that she was also crying in her sleep but always thought that it was a dream until one night she woke up and could not control the tears streaming down her face. The things the doctor had told her were really true after all. The denial and blaming others for whispering behind her back about her condition had all come true. She realized that she had to prepare for the worst. She is going to lose her memory and not just a little but all of it, and this frightens her so much. Now that the tears are really real, and she can now let someone know about the tears, she no longer is afraid of crying because her heart is breaking from fear, and feelings that no one cares have literally made her feel she has already lost her mind. What will be the next stream of events that will hit her mind? Will it be no memory of her children or her husband? Or will it be something as simple as forgetting how to prepare a hot drink or her meal? Will the tears come back and go on and on? Will they terrorize and torment her in all that she does? So she has Alzheimer's. All the horror stories she had heard about other people, she now heard about herself, all the people forgetting their minds, forgetting their names, and so on. *No, no way that would ever happen to me*, she thought. But now reality has set in. She just seems to have self-fulfilled this prophecy and mostly by worrying if she too might get this horrid disease.

Could It Be Prescription?

A lady who had early-onset Alzheimer's and I were sitting around talking about this disease one day. We were talking about what might have started this disease, where it could possibly come from. One thing that she said caught my mind. I don't know if it was meant jokingly. But anyhow this stayed with me for quite some time. She said, "I wonder if all these different medications the doctors are prescribing have something to do with people getting this disease. They prescribe so much stuff you don't know what you're getting, and maybe they're not telling people because of money." Well, I wondered if that could be a possibility. It sure made a lot of sense to me, although I'm sure

I'd get into a huge argument with many people out there on that subject. I by no means am trying to say that this is true. I'm only expressing the view of a very frightened woman who was just searching for answers to this horrible disease, and by speaking with her, I had hoped to help her find some sort of peace in listening to her feelings about something that had her life in a turmoil and was about to throw her normal into madness. And the very thought of that had me in fear even. At any rate, it has given me something to think about, and I'm sure that we aren't the first two to discuss this theory. Alzheimer's is a powerful disease, how it steals a person's memory and won't give it back. And I say won't give it back by means of doctors not having found a way to stop it, only slowing it down, and that has been going on for many, many years. Alzheimer's has many families held hostage, putting their loved one in bondage, and eventually will have the entire family in bondage also—the bondage of struggling each day, praying, or in hoping deeply of getting a phone call one day from someone telling them that they have finally found a cure. Many around the world suffer and are in sadness and misery because of the fact that Alzheimer's may be around for years and years to come just like cancer.

Too Early to Celebrate

Susan was a sixty-seven-year-old with Alzheimer's. She still could fairly do a lot of things for herself. Susan loved to talk and have long conversations with her family and friends. But on this particular day, Susan just happened to hear some of her relatives plan what she thought was the wonderful, beautiful celebration for the end of her life: her death and funeral. *Wow,* she thought, *they are burying me before I was gone.* This made Susan very angry, but she didn't complain or tell her family how this hurt her feelings. Instead, she stewed over it until she was ready to burst. I told her she should definitely speak with them and tell them how this makes her feel instead of letting it eat at her, which was very unhealthy for her. Still, even though she was upset, she was worried about hurting their feelings. I explained again that when she felt up to it, she should tell them while her memory was still intact (not to be insulting toward her). Susan told me how she had overheard her family members laughing about her going away. I tried to assure her that she probably misunderstood them, but she was set on the thought that they were glad to get rid of her. I know that people with Alzheimer's often were confused and make very poor judgments. The family noticed that Susan was becoming more and more withdrawn from them and seemed to not want their company. So they came to me for an explanation, and I explained to them that Susan has it in her mind that her family is planning a going-away celebration for her and was happy about it. Immediately her sister let out a loud laugh and informed me of how they were planning a celebration dinner for their sister, whom they loved very much. And all the laughing came from how surprised they knew she would be when they presented her with this dinner, where everyone who loved her would be there. Since Susan saw me as a good friend and not just a caregiver, she would confide in me most times. So I was left with the job of getting her to the dinner that ended up going better than I thought. Over time and with dealing with different people, I had become very clever with redirecting and getting the ones I cared for to see things my way. In the end, things went great, and Susan had a wonderful time at her dinner.

The Rotting Tree

Alzheimer's is like a tree, she said, nice long fresh vibrant green leaves hanging off the branches. Each day someone makes sure it continuously gets its nourishment so that it will keep its radiant look. Then one day someone stops caring for the tree, and it starts to dry up, and all the green leaves begin to drop to the ground and turn brown. With no one there to get it back to its healthy self, it will continue to wither away more and more until there is nothing left there except a skeleton of what used to be, standing still and quiet with no emotion, no leaves slightly blowing in the breeze on a light spring day. In the end, that skeleton has fallen over and broken down and is unable to retrieve its old self.

Soon you look around, and it's gone, just a stump from what once was. Alzheimer's is a thief. It comes like the devil to steal, kill, and destroy. There is no other ending to it. It only has a sad ending. There are no two stories of how in a few months it will restore itself and return her to that person she once knew. We may as well say our good-byes when that old demon comes sniffing around. There is no restoration or returns, only the long sad good-bye. She said she felt that, like the tree, pieces of her fall off each day, and there is no doctor who can restore or put back together the pieces that are falling off. She felt like piece by piece down to the very last body part, her life will be gone. Her body will vanish right before her eyes. And this really puts a constant recurring fear in her mind. Deep into the night, long into her sleep, she says she can no longer focus on sleep. Even though she goes to bed, she is not resting because her mind is now a movie that plays over and over and can't be stopped. The movie reel goes on and on with no one to stop it or take off the reel, not until she has totally gone away, the ending of herself.

Strength over Me

"Alzheimer's seems to always be there," he said, "every time I try to work on doing something better that I thought I hadn't fully forgotten. It seems to always show up to challenge me as if it were another person, to beat me at a game of golf, a card game. I tried to regain some of my life, some of my memory, but Alzheimer's showed up each time to battle with me and let me know that he will win no matter how hard I try or what fight I put up. I went to the doctor to tell him that I will no longer take the medications, which I felt weren't working one way or the other. Yes, they are supposed to buy my memory a little time, but still they could not save my life. So I continue to have a sparring partner, which I could not see, but I could see the damage and the blows that he had inflicted on me. He was much more powerful than I. He had eyes I could not see, hands I could not feel, but continued to squeeze the memory out of my losing brain. I still decided that I would continue to try to fight this giant, which was much bigger and taller than me. No matter how much fear and anxiety I had going on inside me, I wasn't giving up on myself no matter what the professionals told me. How could I accept this horrible diagnosis? Not me. This could not be me." As time went on, his memory became less and less. It seemed he was going to lose another golf game to this giant. He found that he no longer remembered this giant's name. So this meant that this giant could now have his way with him now. "How can I run now? How can I fight back? I can't remember the tools I used to fight this thing. Finally, I decided to focus on the times that there was no golf game to win, the days when I did have all the cards if just for one day, one week. I decided I would take that time to play that golf game and that game of cards with my family and friends. I know that these folks would play fair with me, and the rest of my days that I did have enjoying games with them would be fun and real, and the rest of my life would be good."

Sick of Technology

He said he was sick of the promises of we are getting closer and closer to a cure for Alzheimer's. "Is this the same thing they have been saying for years and years about cancer? I feel technology is nothing without humanity. Will Alzheimer's spiral out of control at some point?" He meant as far as people not being able to get the care they need because of not having health insurance or money to pay for the care they may need if they should end up with this horrid disease. I don't know what I should be doing or preparing for. I'm sure once my memory is totally gone, some family member will step in and care for me. But what if you don't have anyone? What do you do? Sometimes, he said, he thought that nothing was being done about the cure of this disease. He felt man was more concerned about self-pleasures. As long as he is able to keep pleasure in his life and nothing was affecting him, it didn't matter much, and that's the selfish world we now live in. As horrible as that sounds, it could be true. Many will get this disease and may not be able to do anything about it. He felt that just because of that, it would cause our health care providers to not take too much concern about Alzheimer's because they will become overwhelmed with the number of people turning up with it. As he looked at himself in the mirror, he asked himself quietly, "What if my own family doesn't want to participate in my care? After all, we are not that close by any means. What shall I do? Will I just be caught up in the system like all the many people who are in nursing homes that aren't so good or well equipped to give the kind of care that I would expect? Oh, it's so frightening, a nightmare in which I am anxious to awaken from. Daily, all I seem to do is sit and worry about nothing. Most times I can't even remember what it was I was worrying about. I can still prepare my meals with you as my standby assistant," he told me. "But I would like to be able to do it all by myself. But I know that accidents wouldn't be far behind, so I guess I need you here, don't I?" he said. I responded, "Yes, but aren't you glad that you and I are more like someone that just comes here to boss you around?" We both laughed. He then said, "If I can't depend on my own family, I know that I have you." I quickly answered sure just to give him a little peace of mind so that it wouldn't be so confusing and empty for him. But I knew that I wouldn't be able to do any more than what I was doing because I wasn't family. I too prayed that his family would do right by him and get him the care he needs when that time came because Alzheimer's will get worse. That's one thing you can count on, I told myself, just like all the others that had confided in me and spoke to me about their fears. I knew in the end that that thing called Alzheimer's would soon come, and they would finally come face-to-face with their worst fears; and like most, by this time, they won't really have the mind capacity to really understand what's happening to them. And if Alzheimer's has one good thing about it, I think that would be it. By the time it comes to finally take your entire memory, you no longer have memory anyway.

I Remember, I Forgot

I got out of bed this morning. I knew there was something I had to do. But it had vanished before I could find my shoe. As I stood up, it came back to me. As I put on my shirt, it was once again free. So I started down the hall. It was now breakfast time. I found myself in the kitchen, waiting for my ride. I think I ate breakfast, though I didn't really know. Did I eat or not? I just don't know. As I waited, my ride never came. Oh well, I guess I had myself to blame. I forgot to set the alarm. I guess there will be no work for me today. I'll call my boss anyway. "I'm sorry I didn't make it in today. I really was trying to be on my way." As the person on the other end listened to me, she said, "You've got the wrong number," and she hung up on me. Oh, I was hurt and confused more than you'll know. They told me I had Alzheimer's. I guess I didn't really know.

Forced into Old Age

I'm forced into old age. What can I do? I will no longer be the same as new. I'm forced into old age. I'm still young inside of me. I don't want this, don't need this. I want to be free. Someone told me I have a disease, a disease that has a strong hold on me. Forced into old age—what's wrong with me? This disease I'm told has an unfamiliar strength, a strength so very tight it will not only hold me. It will rub me, kick me, and play tricks on me. It will take my mind and try to steal my soul, mold my heart till it works no more. Make me cry and shut many doors. Steal my name and replace my health with something that's not really worth itself. I'm forced into old age. I want back my youth. I want this Alzheimer's thing to explain why. Why it chose me out of everyone in this world. Doesn't it know I have plans to prevail? Forced into old age—there is nothing I can do. Be careful Alzheimer's don't get you!

CHAPTER 12

How Did I Get Here?

Mary said, "How did I get here? It seems I was just at home with my husband making dinner. And the next thing I know, I'm sharing space with other people. I don't really like being here. I'd rather be home with my husband, preparing dinner." Mind you, she's repeated this twice; and that's because she can't remember she's said it already, typical of a person that has Alzheimer's. She wandered around trying to figure out where her husband was and why he was late for dinner. Her beloved husband has been dead for at least twenty years, but in her mind, he is still alive; and I wouldn't advise you to try to tell her anything different. She searches around her new surroundings, looking for memories of home. The bedroom she's been assigned doesn't look like a place she remembered. She's very sad because she feels alone, even though there are many others there to get acquainted with. But it still wasn't home. She spent her first night at the adult family searching for familiar things and people and, most of all, her husband. It made her very sad that she could not find her husband or anything she recognized. So she retreated to her bedroom and cried most of the night, being comforted by me and other caregivers. Mary refused to accept her new home and made sure we all were aware that she would not be staying. She continuously followed me, asking how she got there and if I could show her the person that brought her there. I repeatedly told Mary that she was there because she could no longer care for herself alone at home. "Well, where is my husband?" she asked again. I had also told her several times that he had been deceased for many years. But she could only respond by telling me I was wrong and must have her husband confused with one of the other ladies' there in the home. Her husband would be along soon. Mind you, you will not win the fight, so do not try please. When you are a caregiver, you have got to be very crafty and patient. Without these talents, you won't last if you're working with people who have Alzheimer's. And I say talent because when you're a caregiver, you must wear many, many hats. Oh, and don't forget the sneakers too. There will be many times when you will need to do a lot of very fast walking or even running.

Mourning My Memory

Jim found out that he had Alzheimer's, and immediately he started to cry. All he could see was the end of his life. He couldn't see anything more than that. Jim became very bitter and withdrawn; he was having a tremendously hard time with his diagnosis. Friends and family could not seem to help or talk to him about anything. This once-vibrant, cheerful, happy man who always had a joke to share became quiet and standoffish. Although he could still do things for himself that would allow him to continue to live in his home, he stopped doing most things altogether such as preparing his meals, changing his clothing, going out to get the mail, etc. When Jim came to my care home, he came very unwillingly, really kicking and screaming. I asked family members to bring as many things that were special to him as possible to maybe make him feel a little better. After a few months, Jim finally settled in and somewhat accepted his new home. I got him to eat meals regularly. Adding some of his favorites sure did help the situation. Jim and I got to know each other pretty well, and he was really a likable guy. But it was very hard to get Jim to come out of his room most times, except for meals. He loved desserts, and I always made sure the folks got a choice of pies and treats after dinner; they were all kind of spoiled at my place. When I finally was able to win a regular relationship with Jim and got him to open up more, Jim would often tell me of how the Alzheimer's had him afraid, and this was why he spent a lot of time in his bedroom. He said he decided to be sad for himself now before his memory left for good. Then he would be like all the other residents happy with Alzheimer's because they no longer knew what happened to their memory, and he would be fine with it then. I told Jim to concentrate on his family now and try to enjoy the memory that he was blessed to have at that moment, to take every day one at a time. When his memory did finally leave him, he would have been having so much fun that he wouldn't remember when it left. We both laughed, and Jim told me that sounded like a great idea.

Borrowed Time

Sara said she felt as if she was borrowing time from God because from a little girl till now, she thought that she would get to spend a certain amount of time on earth, but she just didn't know when that time would end. She now wonders what she can do with the time she feels God has lent to her. She now knows just about when her life would be over. "It's so sad to me," she says. "It leaves me feeling numb and cold. I feel as if I need someone to hold me at all times, just as my mother did when I was a little girl." The two of them could shut out the world and stop time right in the moment they were in and start it back when all the pain and heart was gone. "But where was Mother? Why couldn't she stop time? Why has God limited her time here on earth when she had so much more to do with her life? I need more time," she says. "I don't want anyone to tell me about this disease everyone is saying that I have. I don't want the doctor to tell me about the medications he has that will make life easier. I just want my mommy and time to stand still and things to be the way they used to be. Oh, why can't they?

The time I feel that God has lent me is not good time. I spend most of it crying and counting, counting the minutes each day to my death. Friends and family tell me that it will be okay when I know it won't. Why do people always try to act as if they know how I feel when they really don't, especially when they aren't going through it themselves? How can they? They cannot feel what I feel or read my mind. Sometimes I feel that I am just wasting some of my precious time feeling sorry for myself. But I want my mind back. I want to remember Christmas past and Christmas to come and all the good and fun times I shared with my husband and children. If only God would give me more time, maybe if I pray harder, he will restore all the time that I now face to lose. HELP!"

Running Water

I can hear the water running. I know I am living alone. I don't remember turning it on. I quickly ran into the kitchen, and no water was running. I ran into the bathroom, and it appeared that someone had been preparing to take a bath. I wondered who else was in my home. Was my mother there to visit? Was my husband running a bath? Oh no, they both had been dead for years. It couldn't be them. Whoever it was must have forgotten to turn it off. It's running over onto the floor. Oh, I'll turn it off and find out who it was. After searching the house thoroughly, I found that there was no one there except me. I don't remember starting a bath. Was I losing my mind? Was this thing called Alzheimer's finally showing me the faces I hadn't seen? Is this how it happens? Will I start to forget bit by bit, little by little, the things that usually would come to me naturally? What will it be next? Will I burn my evening dinner? Will I even remember I was cooking my dinner? Will someone find me burned to death in my home one day? Oh, confusion surrounds me. Fear is the only company I have. I don't know what my next move will be. I have no living family that I can count on. I'm all alone. I used to hear folks talking all the time about people having Alzheimer's, and I too would say how sad it was and how lonely it must be. But I never dreamed that I would ever get this disease myself, when the time comes when I will forget I've already put my shirt on and my socks and pants. When will I forget my own name? Will people forget about who I am? Will they want to forget who I am? I hear that Alzheimer's steals your mind and molds your soul. Will I speak the same, or will I mumble? I thought that I would like to take a bath. But I can't remember how to turn the water on at all now. Do I just lie here until the aromas of my flesh spread through my home and my broom and vacuum cannot be used because I no longer know how to use them? What do I do? Where do I turn when the water will not run? (a lady who didn't have help with this disease)

Pauline and the Baby

Pauline was a sixty-seven-year-old female that loved babies and baby dolls. Whenever someone would come for a visit with a child, Pauline would have a difficult time letting go if she was introduced to that child. Sometimes she would cry because she had memories of her children when they were young, and she still thought that her daughter was a young baby girl. So this made it hard for her. Pauline received a baby doll from me to make life easier for her, and every night, she would rock her baby girl to sleep as though it were a real baby. She also carried it around most days as if it were a real child. And none of the other residents were allowed to touch it. One sunny day, as everyone sat out on the deck having a cool drink, Pauline noticed that another resident had her baby doll; and this made her furious. She immediately grabbed this resident's hair and began to pull as hard as she could. There was no way that she was going to allow other residents to handle her doll. After a short scuffle that had to be broken up quickly, Pauline finally got her baby doll back. She started to cry in fear that someone would eventually take her doll away for good. So after hours of convincing, we finally got her back on track. I was comfortable that that would not be happening again. Pauline's children never came to see her, and I think that this is where the fear set in for her. She was a very lonely lady. Before she received the doll, she would follow me around the home and try to help with daily chores that had to be done. And that was my way to resolve that situation. When her children did come, they only stayed for a moment. And that eventually built up a fear in their mother that she had a hard time letting go, you know, the fear of abandonment. When she was diagnosed with Alzheimer's, she became very afraid, as I'm sure most people are. But hers was a little more severe because of the fact that her loved one started to leave, starting with her husband. He decided it was too much for him. Then slowly but surely, everyone just kind of left her to deal with it alone, if not for the state help. God only knew what would become of her (poor lady). Pauline got better eventually. But she always longed for her family who never really showed up at all, not until her death, of course. And I had to track them down even then.

Alzheimer's and Understanding It

A—All the days and nights spent finding and running behind your mind.

L—Trying to do your best when they say it isn't enough.

Z—Zooming in and trying to focus on a mind that's no longer available.

H—Helping those who are no longer able to help themselves.

E—Everyone that comes to visit and don't stay long.

I—Ignoring whispers and judgments that you can do nothing about.

M—Moments embracing bouts of memory that they still have.

E—Emotional times when all you know is fear.

R—Reality of accepting this disease.

S—Staying positive when you know the true outcome.

So many people whom I've cared for with this disease go through the ten things I've listed above. I've been there most of the times to help both the residents and family members with questions and answers if I could. This disease has the ability to tear families apart, and it is in my opinion that all family members should get the education about this disease, which will be so helpful in understanding and caring for their loved one.

It is such a sad and rapid disease that comes in quickly and devastates families in a matter of months. At the same time, it can break families apart and leave the caregiver to suffer if there isn't more than one. You must get your rest and time off if you are a caregiver. Time off is a must. If you don't have another relative to step in and help, you may want to hire help if possible. Doing the care alone will catch up with you and leave you bitter, burnt out, overworked, and extremely exhausted. I know. I've taken care of six all alone for one year. Can you imagine how I felt? Even though this is my passion, I am still human, and by no means did I have superhuman strength. I gave the word "burnout" a new name. As friends said to me, "You must be insane, Brenda."

Please Give Me Something to Do

People with Alzheimer's should always if possible be kept active, keeping their minds fresh and involved in something different. Although it may be something they have participated in before, it may be new to them because it may be something they have long forgotten how to do. I stepped in and took care of Gertrude after her previous caregiver was fired because she spent most of her time watching soap operas or Lifetime television and left Gertrude sitting looking out of the kitchen window with nothing to do. I am very sensitive to seeing that type of thing. It makes me very sad. So when I got there, I had loads of things planned for Gertrude to get involved with, and Gertrude was ready to get into something too. Some caregivers aren't paid well, so they are only willing to match the work with the pay and think that it's fair even if the agency instructed them to do differently. So the client ends up watching the caregiver sleeping off her shift or the caregiver watching the client sleeping, which most times is okay with them (no work). Some clients wouldn't have it any other way than to just sit around doing nothing, not putting their minds into things a little more challenging. I've met plenty of those kinds also. But if you can get them to join in some activity, that would be nice. Gertrude was a nice, quiet, laid-back kind of lady; and she was always ready to do some type of homework. Folding clothing seemed to be something she really enjoyed. But I did board games, puzzles—things like that. We even went outside, weather permitting, to try planting a few simple plants. It was so sad seeing ladies and gents sitting around bored out of their minds because no one would interact with them. It made me start to think I hope that when I'm really up in those golden years, they be golden, not with nothing to do, no one to talk to, or no activity to be involved in. This is why physical activity is so important as we start to age. Remember always: use it or lose it.

Feelings on Getting Old

How do you feel about getting old? Does it bring fear to your heart, or does it bring a sense of accomplishment? Well, for me, it by no means brings fear.

If anything, it brings a sense of getting better and wiser, things past I would have done differently. Gosh, these days all of us who are blessed to reach old age should be thankful. I welcome it with great joy! The only way I would fear it would be if I were to gain an illness that I had to live the rest of my life with, and it will cripple me from doing some of the things that I would like to do in those golden years. I want them to be just that—golden—going as long as my limbs will let me, whether it's traveling or as small as planting in my garden or shoveling snow in the driveway in the winter months. Keeping it moving. Thinking back about the days of my childhood, I was a bit of a tomboy, climbing trees and on top of the garage, riding my bike with no hands, and watching my brothers build hot rod cars from old apple boxes, giving the rest of us a ride by pushing us down the street. Fun days. Do you ever reminisce about your childhood? I sometimes as I've gotten older look at my face each birthday, and as I got older, I would always notice something different about my face: a new line around my mouth area, a wrinkle, or a little sag around my neck area. Either way, I'd always get something new on my birthday. Only it would be a gift I would prefer not to have. But we cannot remain young all the days of our life. When I was a child, my skin was something I never paid much attention to, and I think most children don't. Our skin is generally nice and soft and supple. Usually it's just the use of a little soap and water, and we're out the door. We had skinned knees and a bump on the head while running freely in the wind without a care in the world—we were only children. Isn't it funny how as a child our minds are basically tuned to play and lots of laughter? And when we've gotten much older, we mostly have moans and groans about our aches and pains, telling our friends about them almost as if we are having a challenge to see who has the most aches, pains, or sore spots. I guess this is why we are once an adult and twice a child, from a baby sweet and cuddly to and adult out for adventure and full of life; then it seems we go right back into childhood, needing most of the things when we were just small children: supervision, guidance, care of hygiene, dressing, and sometimes feeding. There you go, right back to childhood, only many years older. Once an adult, twice a child.

Are We Sure?

I've always wondered, I've taken care of so many different types of folks, some with Alzheimer's, some with mental illnesses, some with just mild dementia, you name it, something I'd like to talk a little about later on in my book. I once took care of a man that I just couldn't figure out. I have plenty of experience. But this particular man sat and held conversations better than I. He read book after book but may have had a hard time explaining back to me what he had read. Still, he went through his days just as plain as mine, but his diagnosis was Alzheimer's. I sometimes question the diagnosis some of these elderly folks get. Could it be possible that the doctors themselves didn't know if that person really had it or not and just decided to say that was what it is? I often wonder. I would sometimes catch a miss from this man; sometimes he'd get his words scrambled like eggs, and then other times he's as sharp as a needle. I couldn't quite figure it out. We would go out, and his manners were intact, where most folk with this disease you could most certainly expect to see some sort of action that let yourself, and everyone else, know they had something all the rest of us didn't. Now I'm not a doctor as I have said countless times. But being around these folks day in and out over about thirty years, I probably know just as much. I think that goes for anyone. If you spend enough time around someone, you'll know most of their habits and most things about who they really are. I've taken care of people who had mental illness and supposedly had Alzheimer's too. I wondered, *How could that be?* But when I accepted a man that was diagnosed with both Alzheimer's and mental illness into my home, that info came with him. I guess people can have multiple illnesses, both mental and nonmental. If you can try to imagine the drama that went on during that period he resided in my home—yes, he had to be placed in another home. He was much too much for me to handle (loved the mind games). After a while, I thought something was wrong with me. I didn't know I had the energy it took to care for him, which was quickly taking me down. But the experience was good to have. It's always good to get the wisdom from our older population even if it comes to you sideways, with eight different minds. You can always look deep and find something useful.

The Land of Alzheimer's

To the people in this world with Alzheimer's, even if your mind no longer functions so that you will know that everyone else understands your conversation, I hope you'll know or realize somewhere in your mind before the curtains close and there is nothing but darkness, that your wives, children, mothers, fathers, brothers, and sisters love you just as you are. If you are still aware enough to know that something is there that makes you afraid and you will be lost and alone, let me be one of the first to tell you that the love in your families' heart will be stronger than that demon called Alzheimer's. Although there will be many days of confusion and many days of fear, you are not alone. You're probably wondering why this happened to you, and I will tell you that will be something that you will probably never get an answer to. If you've just newly been diagnosed with this disease and you don't know what to do, I'd like to tell you coming from the heart of a caregiver to try to hold on to the memories that are close to your heart and hold on to them tightly. When they start to fade away, know that there are many people like me whose heart and hands reach out to you and hear your many concerns. I can surely tell you that there are many caregivers out there like me that really care from their hearts. This is something that we do and love doing. Please don't let the true stories in this book make you afraid or shatter your thoughts in any way because I care. This is why I've written this book. Alzheimer's is a horrible disease, but know that you are one of God's great gifts to those who truly love you. And I'm sure that they will be at your side through it all. You may feel that you are in a different land, and no one understands you. Believe me when I say I do. That is why I took interest in such a challenging illness. My heart is open wide to serving and making each and every one of your days as memorable as I can for as long as you can, and life will be as wonderful as you've always remembered it. I too have had this illness that affects people in my life who are close to me. So I can relate to your wife, sister, brother, or mother when they tell me they are afraid, they are sad, they get angry, they get mad—when they tell me they don't know why the person they love so much has to say good-bye. When the words stop making sense and when you say those shoes aren't yours, just remember, you'll do just fine. When you've gotten to the point when there is nothing more to say, just know everyone will love you anyway. So when your mind finally gets to that foreign land, just know we caregivers will hold your hand. Even if you will be in a lost land, there will be people around who understand.

Once an Adult, Twice a Child

Once an adult, twice a child, it's as if you've crossed that mile. Little boys and little girls, coming in and out of our world. Here today, gone tomorrow, leaving everyone with much sorrow. How does one's mind go through the strain, changing from knowing to not knowing a thing? Once an adult, twice a child—can you remember that sweet smile? Swings, candies, and bouncing balls, Mommy taking you to the mall.

Birthday parties, proms, and the high school dance, looking across the room at a boy named Lance.

Husband and wife with children and a home—you never thought that one day you'd be alone.

How time passes by when you're having such fun, family, traveling, visiting everyone. Time passes quickly when you're having fun. Next thing you know, your life has gone.

Once an adult, twice a child—it would be nice just to capture it for a while. One time we're small and one time we're big. Once an adult, twice a child—this is how we live.

Chapter 13

A Little about Dementia

Most of us will experience some type of memory loss as we age, some more severe than others. That's when it becomes a mild type of dementia or more advanced and on its way to Alzheimer's. In my experience giving care, most of the residents who lived with me had very advanced Alzheimer's; they are called heavy care people. These types can really become a huge challenge. Dementia and normal aging are two different types of memory loss. You have MCI, which is mild cognitive impairment. Some believe this is early stages of dementia, or it will progress to full dementia. It seems that everyone has their own diagnosis of what they feel dementia is and what Alzheimer's is, what's mild and what's heavy. Well, I just called it as I saw it. Like it's been said, experience is the best teacher, and that's something that I had a lot of experience in working with these types of folks. Although I've had people with mild dementia too, one thing I know for sure is there is a great difference in the state of mind of someone with Alzheimer's and someone with dementia. From speaking to eating meals, following directions—you name it, there was a great noticeable difference. Conversation-wise, people with dementia just seem to have a problem remembering what they wanted to say, and folks with Alzheimer's don't know what to say at all. They do not even remember how to form the words by mouth or memory. They're in total confusion with plenty of anxiety trying to find the words to say to the point that it really tires them out. Meanwhile, the person with dementia takes a little time, and soon they can usually get their conversation back on track. People who have mild cognitive impairment should be monitored also, but the freedom they have is a lot more than someone with Alzheimer's. About 85 percent of people with dementia will at some point develop Alzheimer's, as statistics show.

Imagine Forgetting

Can you imagine waking up one morning to your normal routine and forgetting all of a sudden what it was? Then you have to sit down for about twenty minutes before you could remember what it was? Well, you're probably experiencing dementia. We all forget. I forget where I parked or where the keys are. But can you imagine the day before you went to work you had a normal day, had lunch with some work associates, and then continued on with your normal day into the evening, had dinner, watched a movie, and finally retired for the night. You had a good night's sleep, and as soon as you sat up, you couldn't move. You didn't know what your next move was going to be or what you had to do. Usually you'd probably go to the bathroom and then wash up, get dressed, and be out to the kitchen for your morning coffee or tea. But here you are still sitting there, and your feet won't let you move because your brain forgot to signal that you're supposed to stand up and go on into the bathroom. So the fear sets in, and suddenly you're overwhelmed about not knowing what to do. Soon after being there for a while, you finally remember what to do, but you're still frightened about what just happened to you. What would you do? Just what would you do? Would you attempt to try to get ready to go to work? Or would you call your best friend or family member to let them know what you just experienced and wonder if it will come back again later, as if it were some type of monster out to take your soul? Scary, isn't it?

Well, I am quite certain that this is what happens to most folks who experience first signs of dementia and Alzheimer's, and my heart stretches out to them very much. I'm somewhat sure your memory bank isn't just gonna go that quickly. But it probably feels that way to the person who just experienced this.

Risk Factors for Dementia

Seventeen percent of women and 9 percent of men fifty-five years in age, people who are insulin resistant, with diabetes, hypertension, obesity, elevated cholesterol, sedentary lifestyle, and lack of exercise, are at risk. Some other things maybe family history, genes, head injury, history of depression. All these things heighten the risk factors. There has been a decline in older people who are taking statin drugs, lowering it by 40 percent in a study in 2008. I've always been a strong believer that exercise and fitness is a good source of medicine for all people, whether it's walking, running, swimming, etc. And if you are homebound, you can always find something to do inside your home. Reading keeps the mind fresh, especially if you feel as though your memory is slipping. Trying to read fifteen to twenty minutes per day should help tremendously. I believe it can even slow down the process. Puzzles and word games are all good sources for keeping the mind fresh if you ask me. Again, I'm not a doctor. But it just seems to me if you're able to still do some reading, then you should be able to go on reading for a while. Walking is something that is good. Just walking and taking in the fresh air and views usually somewhere where there are lots of flowers and trees can keep the mind focused and remembering different things. People with Alzheimer's are far busier than those with dementia even when they are still. Can you imagine that? Their mind is usually still going. Dementia is somewhat laid-back, if I can say it that way without prejudice. Believe me, I am just trying to explain it so you, the reader, can think about this with a loved one or someone you know with Alzheimer's. Both of these diseases are sad and difficult, and having dealt with both, I thought I'd try to give you a little insight. Alzheimer's has been demanding of most of my time over the years. Anyway, I hope that I have enlightened you a little on this disease.

Dementia/Alzheimer's

Dementia/Alzheimer's is after me. Please, someone, come help set me free.

Oh god, why such a confusing disease? One that constantly has me down on my knees. Tearful nights and lonely days, no one likes my different ways. Don't they know that this is not me? I'm not the way I used to be. Don't be ashamed when my conversation ain't right. Don't roll your eyes or get uptight. When I was like you, with mind still intact, I never saw you act like that. I wish sometimes I could just run away. I think of it each and every day.

Alzheimer's/Dementia

Alzheimer's/dementia—this is blowing my mind. I can't even remember how to tell the time. Slowly one day, when I was feeling blue, I thought to myself, "I'd like to be new." The power to just change the way I am, transform myself into a healthy man. Strong and vibrant—oh, with muscles too. I just can't figure out what to do. The doctor said it wouldn't go away or just forget about me one sunny day. Instead he said it would always stay by me, holding on tight so I can't go free.

Am I going out of my mind? That's what some will say. They'll gossip with their friends when I'm gone away! I guess there is nothing I can do, but realize this is me, not you. So when your lips can no longer speak of me.

Just remember now I am free, free from the burden of what's to come, free from not knowing anyone, free from all the stares and whispers around me, free from this lonely, ugly disease.

So, my friends, please think of me when you see someone with this disease. Instead of staring or whispering so free, try to be kind and wish them glee.

A Little on Mental Illness

What is mental illness? To tell you the truth, I really do not know. All that I can say is I've worked with several who have been diagnosed with this disease by a doctor. Could it be that most of us may have a little mental illness in us? Could it be depending on how far one is pushed before you can really witness it? Or is it considered mental illness because it's a continuous thing? Several things can aggravate a person with this disease and set their illness off. Hmm. I wonder. The Surgeon General of the United States says that one in every five Americans may experience mental illness in any given time of the year. Mental illness like Alzheimer's is a brain disorder that affects a person and his or her relationship with others. Alzheimer's is not being so violent at all times.

Many doctors believe that mental illnesses have chemical basis. This I can see as believable if you watch someone who has been, say, an alcoholic for a greater part of their lives. They seem to eventually get a mental illness, and you can identify it just by their actions, intoxicated or not. They seem to have psychosis (meaning loss of touch with reality). Most have psychotic outbreaks. Most are short but can be very scary for those not aware of seeing that sort of thing, causing some to go right into a defensive mode, fearing for their safety. That to me would be a good thing to do. Most of the time, psychotic breaks would be hard to identify, or predict, and could happen at any time. People with mental illness have problems thinking logically or remembering things; they are easily confused. Although I've had experience with several types of mental illness, I must say that there were a lot of times where I was very frightened to have that person in my home; as some would say, I was sleeping with one eye open. If you have a loved one with this disorder, try to be a good listener and very understanding. Even if you don't agree, keep it to yourself. Some people with mental illness get offended very easily. So be careful not to judge.

Anxiety

Mental illness brings on an awful lot of anxiety. Anxiety is the fear that something bad is going to happen and seeing no end to what it could be. It's not like being anxious. We all get anxious whether it's from paying bills, taking a test, or just worrying about daily challenges that may come, such as home repairs or as simple as what to fix for dinner. I myself feel that if you suffer for longer than a year, anxiety may turn into mental illness because that's way over six months. Now it's become more severe and can really interfere with the normal life you should be living. Most of the folks I cared for that had Alzheimer's were very anxious but were given medications for it. Anxiety can ruin one's life if he or she lets it, and I'm speaking to all the normal people out there that seem to let the small things take them to a place where they're trapped and mentally cannot leave. At my care home, I also had a very young lady whom I was told just had physical handicaps, but besides that, she was normal. After having this young lady for about two weeks, I really started to see other issues, like mental issues. She cried continuously day in day out; and when you asked her what was wrong, all she said was "I don't know." I knew then that there were some serious mental or anxiety issues with her that were not told to me. She finally opened up. Apparently, her mom had told her not to reveal what was so ugly hiding inside her head. I guess crying was somewhat a way to soothe her tormented mind and the ongoing memories of being sexually abused by her stepdad. This young girl was only eighteen. I can imagine the anxiety and fear she had inside her. I told her that I would get her help and that she probably wouldn't be going back to the home where her mother would allow the boyfriend to molest her own child who was handicapped. This really hit home with me, and I made it my business to put her torments to rest and her parents in jail where they belonged. I hoped that in jail they could get to find out what it was to be tormented and filled with high anxiety.

What Do You Do if Someone You Love Has Two Diagnoses?

I've taken care of a few people who I was told had one diagnosis, which I found to be untrue later on. I don't know why they felt they had to lie to me, but they did. This particular person had dementia and severe mental illness, and by the time I finished caring for her, I too almost had a mental illness. Boy, did she send me through the loops. Some will have you thinking there is something wrong with you. If you're someone who has two illnesses, you truly have my blessings. This will really be a tiring and drilling experience to contend with. You should be sure that you are getting your rest and meals right and on time. You will truly be overwhelmed with stress, sometimes even if you have someone sharing the care with you. That one person could make it seem as if there are three or more people you're taking care of. If one of the illnesses is substance abuse, you're probably really in for a ride. They will do almost anything to get the drug of their choice so that along with a mental illness, it will send you on a roller-coaster ride. And these two disorders together are the worst combinations if you ask me. If you are trying to keep their drugs from them and they insist on taking them without your assistance, or stay on a schedule with their medications, you may be in trouble. They will become very combative and won't hesitate to hurt you to get what they need. So with that said, now may be a good time to really seek professional help. Denial is something that will take a long time for them to admit, so if it were me, I would certainly be gentle with this person and show them much love. You can catch more flies with sugar than salt. Know that you cannot and will not ever stop them from quitting their addiction. They need the professionals to help them with their problem. All you can ever do is give all your support. Don't be a nag and certainly do not be tricked into using with them. Try to get help for both disorders if possible. Kill two conditions with one stone, and hopefully you can finally get a little relief.

What You Can Do to Get Help

A lot of the time the person with the mental problem may be ashamed of their disorder. If you are caring for someone with, say, Alzheimer's/mental illness, maybe you may want to help him/her. Start with a journal. Jot down their daily activities from morning till the end of their day. This should be something you should sit down and do together when it's pretty quiet, making it clearer to remember what occurred through the day. Date each page and time. This will be a good way also to see if there are any changes good or bad. Include any experiences you may have had that were upsetting for you. After about a week or two before your doctor's appointment, review it for any changes and take this info to the doctor's office so he can review it too. Together you may be able to resolve some of the more serious problems. Mental illnesses come in cycles sometimes, and you may be fooled into thinking it's over, but this is only a relapse. It will come back soon. But the biggest difference you could make in someone who may be a substance abuser is to try to stop that type of abuse first. A lot of the time when a relapse happens, that person may think it's okay to stop taking their medication also. Stressful events, drug use, and changes in medications can all cause relapses. If a time comes when you think a relapse may be coming, you should call your doctor ASAP. You should always have a crisis plan set up and carry it with you at all times: phone numbers to doctor's family members, etc. Always try to eat healthy fruits and vegetables. Try to stay clear of sugars and junk food and drink lots of water. In the end, try to take care of that person as best you can; and if you cannot, make sure you research some of the best care homes around to ensure that your loved one gets the best care they possibly can get from a reputable care home.

Caregivers, Take Care

When you're caring for a loved one, it's really easy to forget about your own needs. Neglecting your own health can be very dangerous resulting in depression, anxiety, and even heart problems. Here are a few things you can do to help take care of yourself:

Find a good support group.

Make sleep a priority.

Do something for yourself every day.

Get moving. Work out if possible.

Practice relaxing.

Stay on top of your own checkups.

Share tasks.

Find time for friends and other family.

Caring for any and all these types of folks can be an overwhelming challenge. Make sure that you take advantage to do the things on the list above for yourself and especially for your health. You don't want to get run-down on your own energy. By then who will take care of you? I know all too well about burnout. When that hits, sometimes there's no turning back to that old life you're used to.

When depression sets in, it may become hard to turn back, and you'll find yourself almost as depressed as the person you're trying to help. So be careful.

Remembering Back Long Ago

I can remember when I was an owner of my care home and taking care of those six residents. The first six months were a piece of cake. I really enjoyed it. But soon after that, I began to feel depressed and very tired. The anxiety set in, and I was overwhelmed with total body breakdown. I remember right before I shut down, I was just so tired I said I hope I never see another elderly person. Don't get me wrong. I said that with love. I just didn't want to do anything but lie down and sleep for a year.

I mean I could have slept standing up. My face was dragged down, and I felt ten years older than I was physically. Everything hurt from lifting people in and out of the bathtub, lugging laundry up and down the stairs—you name it. When it came to house work, I was doing it all. This is why I stress so much about caring for yourself. Anxiety can take over, and after a while, you will start to feel sickly yourself. Then you will end up sick, and who will take care of them if there's no one else? Try to realize if you're needing help with your mental health. Are you having problems making decisions? Feeling lonely? Feeling like crying all the time? Feeling unhappy most of the time? Don't have any relationships or anything that is fulfilling? You get angry very easily for no particular reason? You can't sleep, or sleep too much? Family members become concerned about your behavior? All these things and a few others unmentioned may help you in finding out if you are on your way to having a mental problem or by now already have one. Noticing highs and lows can really confirm also that you may have a mental problem.

If all the above is happening to you, then you are probably getting toward having a mental breakdown. When I got burned out so badly, it sparked anger in me. I was lucky that I didn't have a nervous breakdown. I came quite close. But the good thing was that I caught it in time and recognized what was happening to me.

Posttraumatic Stress and Lynda

Lynda was a thirty-two-year-old female that came to me for care when I ran my care home. Although my home was basically for people with Alzheimer's, for some reason, I opened my heart up to this lady. But with the amount of issues she had, there would be days when I found it hard to believe that this lady was getting through her days so happily. She just made herself at home with me right away and wasn't one bit ashamed to tell me about the traumatic stress. She had been through an awful lot. I think all the laughs she had was to hide the cries. Posttraumatic stress is a combination of many things. Many things could have happened to her in her life that caused her much grief and sadness: car crash, domestic violence, natural disasters, rape, etc. These things are very hard for many people to deal with, depending on the age. Most have the hardest time dealing with this disorder when they're older in age. Lynda had been raped, beaten, and made to do many ugly things with a family member. Although she hid away most of her feelings, I knew that she was in a lot of pain mentally. I grew very concerned about all the medications she was taking for her disorder; at least that's what she expressed to me, that they were prescribed. There would be many days when she was very angry with us and many days when she was very depressed. I often talked with her hoping it could somehow soothe her. I felt in my heart she was abusing some sort of narcotic or some other drug besides the ones prescribed by her doctor. There were times when I couldn't identify some of her moods, being that I had become familiar with most of them. Lynda was really loose with the men. I couldn't understand how she could be like that after she had been raped. Well, in the end, Lynda left my place when everyone was sleeping one evening, leaving most of her belongings. Many months went by before

I found out her whereabouts. When I did, I found that she was in one of the local mental institutions in our town and wasn't doing too well. I think she may have had a mental breakdown, and that was the last I heard of her. So you see, many different disorders are out there, and taking on too much can sometimes have a very bad effect on you if you're not careful to take care of yourself.

In the End

In the end, all my family and friends, I hope that this book will bring you comfort within. I hope you find peace in that place way down in your soul.

I hope that your loved one never grows old. I hope that your journey down through these pages from my soul will bring you peace and let you know that no matter how hard the struggle is, Alzheimer's/dementia can be your friend.

To win this fight, you must be calm because your loved one won't have too long.

Love them, hold them, and tell them, "I love you." Tell them not to be afraid when they no longer know you.

It has been a pleasure serving you, making sure your loved one gets through, through all the pain, the tears, and the joy, through the moments of forevermore.

I wish I could make this horrible thing just go away, but I'm just a caregiver each and every day.

Take their love with you, on that sad and lonely day, know they'll live in your heart, and that's where they'll stay.

Just hold on to the good times of yesteryear, the laughs, and smiles, when there were no tears.

As their caregiver, they became my best friends. I too knew I'd never see them again.

This breaks my heart as much as it does yours, but I will continue to open my doors.

A pathway to happiness if only for a short while, I'll remember the laughter and all the great smiles.

So if anyone is faced with this different kind of identity, just remember it could be you or me.

So as I say so long to all my friends, I leave you this book and all my love within. You've left your footprint deep in my heart. And somehow I know we shall never part.

So, so long to all the ladies and gents. Maybe one day we will meet along the way. Dedicated to all the sweet women and men that I've taken care of over the years, thanks for taking your time to get to know me. It's been an honor and a journey that I shall never forget. So long, my friends, so long.

Brenda Johnson

A very special thanks to a great friend, Danielle Ezzard, for encouraging me to write this book. You will never be forgotten.

About the Author

Brenda Johnson was born in the great northwest in a small town named Yakima Washington. The youngest girl with eight siblings, Brenda always felt the need to care for her brothers and sisters and anyone else who needed help. From a very young age she loved caring for others and has dedicated most of her life doing so. She successfully ran a care home for six people whom had the disease Alzheimer's, most times giving care to six elders who could not care for themselves alone. It has been a passion that Brenda has found very hard to discontinue. So she has gone on to write books, and other creative ideas to ensure her continued involvement doing what gives her the most pleasure. She has given care to many mom and dads through the years, and is greatly appreciated for the care and kindness she has given from many grateful children of those stricken with this horrible disease. She wishes to get the word out to those who are not informed about Alzheimer's, and hopes that people would get more knowledge of the disease and understand the devastating affects it can have on a family. she sends many prayers to anyone whom has to deal with a love one whom has fought this fight over the years, and ask that they stay strong loving and most of all a friend and family to those who may no longer remember your face. May God bless you.

466-8782

Marxism - breakdown of family
BLM - Marxist, leftist group
moral decision of the progressive left,
Marxism is here - will we wake up ?
" is anti-biblical
   as sovereign God
      there are - goals
Scrippt